SPEAK TO A FORTUNE

Make a fortune teaching what you love

ARFEEN KHAN

SPEAK TO A FORTUNE

Make a fortune teaching what you love

Om Books International

First published in 2019 by

Om Books International

Corporate & Editorial Office
A-12, Sector 64, Noida 201 301
Uttar Pradesh, India
Phone: +91 120 477 4100
Email: editorial@ombooks.com
Website: www.ombooksinternational.com

Sales Office
107, Darya Ganj,
New Delhi 110 002, India
Phone: +91 11 4000 9000
Fax: +91 11 2327 8091
Email: sales@ombooks.com
Website: www.ombooks.com

ISBN: 978-93-5276-712-0

Printed in India

10 9 8 7 6 5 4 3 2 1

For

All the Transformational Experts, Speakers,

Trainers, and Coaches

who have played the awesome role of being a Superhero,

and have helped millions of people out there!

Dear Reader,

Before you think this is just some random self-help book, stop! This is what I have done and what I love! If you have ever thought that speaking is hard, the systems I use will instantly help you become an ace speaker. If you ever thought finding clients is difficult, I will show you how you can generate unlimited leads online.

You will certainly get something out of *Speak to a Fortune*, not the typical 'do this, do that', but lessons that will make you a better person when you are done. And which shall stay with you for a long time!

I would like to thank Ajay Mago, my publisher and Dipa Chaudhuri, Chief Editor, Om Books International, and Dhwani Davda for their efforts in putting together this book.

Enjoy the read.

Contents

Introduction

My name is Arfeen Khan and, for the past 25 years, I have been in the field of personal transformation. I started off purely by chance. There was a time I didn't know what I was going to do. So, one day, I became a salesperson selling water filters–that's what I used to do. I was a water filter salesperson and at that time, there was a bottled water revolution and bottled water was launched globally. It was promoted as an image product–if you want to be cool and classy, drink bottled water. In fact, tap water was promoted as being deadly to drink.

Bottled water took off. Bottled water companies did awesome marketing to shift everyone to bottled water. But bottled water was very expensive – it was more expensive to drink bottled water than to use petrol at that time. Then someone came up with the ingenious idea of creating a water filter, but marketing it as an in-house bottled water system, not a water filter.

Fresh bottled water on tap sounds really good and that's exactly what bottled water is–filtered water in a bottle. We all know that, right?

So, I started selling that but wasn't a very confident, so I underwent training as a salesperson with my brother Shez who was already a fine trainer. I used to watch him and think, 'This guy is amazing; will I ever be like that?'

One day, there was a programme for 150-200 people in Central London and my brother came on stage and said, 'Ladies and gentlemen, I am going to introduce you to Arfeen Khan who's going to take you through the fast start training.'

Now, I was backstage and dying thinking 'What the hell do I do? Do I exit or do I face it,' but of course, this was my brother, I couldn't embarrass him, so, I didn't go on stage because I wanted to, but because I had no choice. I just had to.

I arrived on stage and started speaking. I was terrified and petrified and I knew nothing. To cut a long story short, I managed to do the training programme and I got great feedback! So, I was truly excited. This is how I started. You, however, don't have to go through all that. Just read on and I'll save you ten years.

Let me fast forward to now. It's been a little over 25 years that I have been a trainer. 600,000 people have heard me speak–an impressive number. And I have done rather well. I have received testimonials from Anthony Robbins, Amitabh Bachchan, Hrithik Roshan, Arnold Schwarzenegger, Brian Tracy, Bhaskar Das, Ex. *Times of India*, Indu Jain, *Times of India,* C.P Krishnan Nair the owner of The Leela Hotels, Palaces and Resorts, to name a few. I have got about 50 testimonials from the biggest names globally. My book *The Secret Millionaire Blueprint* has a fantastic Foreword by the very famous Indian actor, Hrithik Roshan. I have acted in a Bollywood movie and my goal is to help at least one million people transform their lives within two years. I have worked with over 100 companies and CEOs; I coach some of the most incredible people on earth.

Today is going to be a different day for you because I am going to tell why I wanted to write *Speak to a Fortune* and how it can be your ultimate guide – not just on how to become a coach/consultant/speaker or an expert, but this book also offers lessons that I have learnt in my life, lessons that have helped me begin and succeed on this journey.

When I decided to write *Speak to a Fortune*, I decided this book would not be about giving you content. Everyone collects content. They feel good about it for a while and then do nothing with it. I am outcome-driven. So, I believe that good speakers, trainers, coaches and even writers, should be outcome-driven too.

1

Can I Do It?

What could be the outcome of this book? What I have discovered is that when a person comes on stage for the first time, they are very nervous, but using the simple systems I have created, they can get rid of all of their nervousness immediately. While that may seem unimaginable, that can truly come to you effortlessly.

When one of my 'Speak To a Fortune' participants Rinku came to her first 5-day event that we had in Goa, India, she was nervous. She was crying her eyes out. She kept asking, 'Can I do this? Can I do this?' But today, she is an awesome and a powerful speaker. She asked me, 'What should I talk about?' I told her, 'Talk about something you love in your life. Talk whatever you want to talk about, it doesn't matter.'

She worked on her mind with me and transformed instantly – as though at the snap of a finger. She keeps giving me credit for it. The actual truth is she had a desire and a willingness to learn and followed my system.

Ultimately, everyone reading this book is going to gain knowledge. Some of you are going to take it and run with it, and others may not. Some of you will take your time, there is no rush. But ultimately, if you follow the system that I am going to share with you, that'll ensure that you will succeed. But you need to take action.

And what you discover over the rest of the pages is that your thoughts are who you become! And the quality of your life is based on the quality of your thoughts – that's the truth. There is nothing more to it. No rocket science. I see people struggling all the time: somebody wants to become a business person, another one a speaker, an actor, etc. For anything you really want to do, your success, your failure shall all be determined by the way you think.

I came out with this book is because I feel the most important reason people fail has nothing to do with content, delivery, how you speak, etc. How you think about yourself and who you are as a person will either stop you from achieving something or propel you to amazing heights.

You need to know your outcomes, be crystal clear about them. When I get on stage, I am clear about my outcome. I know that over a period of time, I'll accomplish my outcome. If you are clear about your outcome, you can do a programme or seminar without almost any preparation. Can you do a full one-day programme without any preparation? Most people can't but if your outcomes are clear, the brain finds a way!

If you can't go on stage and speak effortlessly, it's because of the way you think, your inner beliefs about yourself. It has nothing to do with your memory retention or your knowledge or what you can do. If you work on your inner thoughts and reframe them, you will never need training on how to speak. When you speak to people about something you are 100 per cent sure of, do you get nervous? NO, because you are sure of yourself. Change your thoughts to change your life.

Right now, do you believe you could sell a $3000 coaching programme or a two-lakh rupees coaching programme? Most will say, 'You are nuts.' The truth is if you follow my system, within 90 days you can have so much clarity about your course outcomes that you will be jumping up and down wanting to speak to people. You may think people will not buy into your outcomes. They will if they know you believe in yourself and in what you are offering. Instead of asking, 'Would they pay me that?' ask, 'What can I do to provide ten times the value of what I charge or what can I do to get people to know that they would be nuts not to hire me? You need to ask if your personal story is powerful enough to charge that amount. People buy your story before they buy your course. I have a ninety-days system that helps you build your online and offline story to make people want to queue up to meet you.

So, the point I am making is, it has got nothing to do with what you are going to develop, because that is secondary. It's about the person who comes on stage. Someone like Tony Robbins didn't come from a rich family, wasn't educated or formally trained. Yet he is brilliant because he has a great story and people flock to him because an ordinary man became extraordinary.

When we were in Africa, he told me that he had a burning desire to help people. He said, 'I was born for this.' He also said that initially he had no belief but just wanted to help and would do anything to find a way to make his story so great that the whole world would learn from it. His belief and dedication speak for themselves.

How is it possible that someone like Hrithik Roshan can dance so well while someone like Salman Khan can't dance as well? Yet, dancing is something that anyone can learn, right? Salman could learn dancing and become a great dancer but will not have the flow like Hrithik Roshan would. Mentally Hrithik loves dancing and his brain cells can't wait to entertain the world. Hrithik is a dancer in his head first, then he's a dancer on stage. The goal is to start getting excited in your head about becoming a speaker, a coach. You must get your brain cells excited to the point that you don't know any better.

Anyway, I was wondering what stops people from achieving what could be the outcome of this book? And how can this book go beyond helping you in your training career, your speaking career, your writing career? What about your life? How can this book help you in a way that can make a big difference?

If the quality of your life is bad and you hope to be a speaker, trainer or coach, it's going to be really hard. The reason is simple – when you go on stage and speak to people, at the back of your mind you shall be saying to yourself, 'Oh my god, what's happening to my life? It's really hard.'

So, I wondered what to think about, what to focus on today that would produce useful results in all spheres of our life. I thought about the inner voice everyone has, why it exists, and where it is.

It's in your head. And it is playing constantly; it does not rest. And some of you would have a very loud and destructive inner voice. Other would have a very loud voice which is constructive, but it could also be destructive, because if the voice is too loud and too positive, even that is bad.

Some might call it ego or arrogance or whatever. There has to be a way to manage that inner voice, tame it, tone it down. So, I am going to share with you today what I do with my clients. I am going to take you through a small process, a small system and hopefully by the end of the day, I will tone down your inner voice a bit, so you can tone it down further.

Your inner voice can become your friend. Whenever you are going through a difficult time and you start berating yourself, or someone attacks you and you start thinking too much about it, you need to tone down the inner voice. So, when you come on stage, your voice will be saying, 'Will you be able to do it? What will happen if you can't? What if people don't sign up? What if people don't register? What if people don't buy it?' From your head, the voice spreads to your body. We need to tone down that voice. And the moment you tone it down, everything becomes effortless.

How many of you have a negative inner voice? Be honest! How many of you don't have a negative inner voice? How many of you are in between? Let's get it right, there is no in-between if you are just trying to defend yourself.

Either you have got a positive voice or you have got a negative voice. And if you have got a positive voice in your head, you will do great things. And if you have got a negative voice, imagine you have just ended a relationship and now you are getting into a new one, you shall carry a voice review and wonder: 'Will this person be the same as the person I left? What if they cheat me? What if they leave me?' Imagine you are going to be in that situation. You are going to be in a certain career, in a certain industry, with the same force, with the voice saying, 'What if I fail? What if no one believes me? Will I do it? Will I be successful? How will I do it? What should I do? How will it work?' These voices continuously playing in your head are going to affect the delivery of what you are trying to produce. Does that make sense?

Yes or No?

Yes!

So, yes, everyone has a negative or positive voice or maybe the word I should be using is everybody has a constructive or a destructive voice. Some people need pain to motivate them and some people need pleasure to motivate them. Either one or the other is more dominant. If you want to be motivated by your constructive voice, and want to take action, then you need to check my Speak To a Fortune Home Study Course, where you can follow your passion and make a fortune out of it! Go to speaktofortune.com/letter to know more!

The Power of your Inner Voice

I used to be pain-driven and now I am more pleasure-driven. Earlier it was: 'Arfeen Khan, if you don't do this, you are going to be in trouble', and my inner voice would say: 'Get lost, I am not doing it.' But if you come and say to me,

'Arfeen if you do this, and this is the possibility,' I will go all out to do it.

The only problem with pain is that some people have such a high threshold of pain that they can take many nonsense from people before they actually make a change. This seems true of some women that I know. If they are in a relationship, and things are bad, they wait till the end, till they can't handle it anymore and then they take action.

For example, I know of women who have been beaten by the husband for over 10 years and they still think, 'He will change, he is lovely guy and he really loves me.' And I want to tell them, 'What the hell are you doing?' But their threshold of pain is very high and one day when the pain gets unbearable, they finally say, 'You know what? I hate this man.'

And I heave a sigh of relief and say, 'You should've said so 10 years ago.'

Men, on the other hand, can't seem to take pain at all – that could be one reason women give birth and men don't. A women's threshold of pain seems to be much higher than that of a man.

I can tell by your body language what's on your mind. So, when I put somebody on stage, just by their body language I can say what is going on in their head. For example, if a person comes on stage and is standing with their hands folded, I understand that they are wondering, 'Why did I come on stage? What if I goof up? What is the audience going to think of me?'

Other people might be very comfortable. They will come on stage, speak and not care of what people think and they will be very confident in their space. They probably might be thinking: 'Let us show these people how good I am at this.' They might take it as an opportunity to have an impact on the audience.

The inner voice does not necessarily have to be negative; it can be very constructive.

Amongst others, I have had the privilege of working with extremely talented, famous and rich people. When you meet some of them, you probably think they should not be doing what they are doing. How could they be so wealthy? The way they are, the way they speak...but I discovered that most people I have met have a very constructive inner voice.

Sometime back, I met a businessman, in fact, a diamond dealer. I know this man and his family very well and have always found them to be nice and simple. They have this two-three nice cars. Once, I went to this huge wedding organised by them in Bali where they had invited a huge crowd of 2000 people. They had flown everyone across to Bali, and provided them all the amenities there.

A few years later, they had the option of organising another wedding in Mauritius or of going for a simpler wedding and saving a crores of rupees. So, they settled for the simpler wedding saving themselves crore of rupees which they then donated to charity. What an amazing thought. Every year he donates to the charities; he has also constructed a huge lake in his village.

He once told me, he had started as a diamond polisher earning just Rs 2500 a month. So, he is someone who has gone from earning Rs 2500 a year to becoming the billionaire that he is today. Well, what made him do that? His simplicity!

The point is, if you meet him or his family member on any given day, anything is possible. They had a floating wedding reception on a lake; crazy as that may sound, they made it possible. What a waste of money you may say; they should spend more money on charity than on themselves. Let me tell you, the entire family eats together; there is no TV in the house, and they play many games together. All their inner voices are really very powerful. So, what I have realised is, people who are really very successful have some level of control over their inner voice and that's going to determine whether you become super successful or not.

Who doesn't know of the superstar Hrithik Roshan, a very good friend of mine. But how many of us know of the kind of challenges people go through in life? Doctors had told him that he wouldn't be able to dance anymore because a part of his knee was badly injured. But in his mind he said, 'No one is ever going to stop me from dancing.' And despite his doctors telling him he was not going to dance, he is still dancing today and brilliantly at that.

If you look around you, you have got several examples of people going from being nothing to being something. What makes them different? Their inner voice – it's got to be that, because the world is pretty much the same for all of us. If you look at the opportunities, they are pretty much the same for all of us. What can be the difference? That you may have less money than somebody or that you may come from a richer family, but the truth of the matter is that everybody can go out there and DO something.

If you look at Shahrukh khan, he came from a non-filmy background and is now amongst the richest actors on Earth, far ahead of even some top-ranking Hollywood actors. How is it possible that he can do that? The world is the same for him too…What makes the difference? Some of you may become the best and the most famous speakers, trainers or coaches in the country or maybe in the world. Maybe a year from now, some of you will be better known than me, maybe you will have bigger audiences than me. Maybe ten time bigger. Who can tell? We don't know, but there's an opportunity out there. And if there's anything that's going to stop you, it's your inner voice.

Look at your past. What are the things that you have not done very well? Think about it – your relationships, your health, your business, your work, your family members, your disputes…Also ask yourself a question: how many of these happened because of that inner voice? Think about it. What about if you got into a relationship, and then you got into another one and then another one and then you realised that every time you entered into a relationship, you were finding the same kind of idiot and it seemed to keep appearing in the same kind of form. That is because you were carrying your previous relationships with you and that inner voice saying, 'For me to manage my life is the most difficult part.'

I have worked in a movie called *Mere Brother ki Dulhan* (2011).Some of you must have seen it. I was told it was a coaching assignment, but when I landed up there, they said to me, 'This is an audition.' Instantly the voice in my head went, '*You are crazy! You can't do it! How can you do it? You are not an actor, you have got work! You are at Yash Raj! Oh my God, it's a big movie production house! Don't do it! Don't do it!! Don't do it!!!*'

And then I told myself, 'Okay, let me at least hear them out.' Then they told me, 'The role is about an autistic guy.' Again the sirens went off on in my head, 'Are you crazy?' And then they told me to look at Dustin Hoffman in *Rain Man* and that I needed to do something similar. I was having a heart panic attack, my head thinking of bailing out, that there was no chance, that I couldn't be stupid, that my whole training career would be destroyed, and if I did a bad job, everybody would say, 'What an absolute loser!' No, I should not be doing this.

And then I told myself, 'Okay let me look at it differently. What if I did it? And what if I succeeded and what would that mean to me?'

First of all, I would be in a Yash Raj movie, and that would be pretty cool. Secondly, I would be with Katrina Kaif. Unfortunately, I would be her brother in the movie but

I would be with Katrina Kaif. And at that time Katrina was the No.1 heroine, and I said this was a good enough reason for me to do this movie. Bollywood, and maybe a billion people would start recognising me.

That evening, I went home and told my wife, 'I don't think I am going to do it.' And she said, 'Are you crazy? People are trying to get through that door for years, just to that door, and to that movie, and you are rejecting it all?' And I said, 'I am not interested. I don't want to deviate.' But the truth was, I was interested! I had been lying all this time. I am revealing that today. But I was scared. What if I went and did one Bollywood movie and it turned out to be bad? But then I composed myself and said, 'Let me do it. I don't want to do it because I want to be an actor. I have no desire to be an actor in any form, ever.' But I told myself, 'What a great way to get publicity. Because actors are big.'

So, when I went for my audition, my whole mindset had changed. I said, 'Okay, what do I do?' I said to myself, 'The audition can't be that difficult.' I went in there and I did it effortlessly. Two days later, they called me and told me 'Congratulations! You got the role.' And even then, I was telling myself, 'No you haven't, she's lying. How can they give you this role? You are not even an actor' and then she told me that 40 people had auditioned for this role and I had got it.

And here my brain was saying, 'Bullshit…liar…I don't believe you.' Because my brain just wouldn't believe it had happened. It was just not possible, given the struggles people go through I have heard that, some people have struggled for 10, 11, 12, 13, 14 or 15 years just trying to get through the door of Yash Raj Films.

And then I said to myself, 'Wow this is a good thing.' But what couldn't stop was my brain. I could've gone to the audition, thinking: 'I am not going to do it. I won't do it,

I can't do it. How will I do it? What if I fail? What if I can't be an autistic person? What if I don't get it right?' So, the media used to always ask me, 'Was it difficult?' And I always used to say, 'No, it was very easy.' And the director used to say, 'No, don't say that. Say it took much courage, a lot of difficulty and months of practice.' But in reality, it didn't.

The only practice I did was I went to Lokhandwala high-street as an autistic person. I went to every shop to see if they could distinguish if I was autistic or not. That's all that I did. It wasn't difficult, because in my head, it wasn't difficult.

I believe, be it anything in your life, if you want to become outstanding or want to become extraordinary, you have got to calm your inner voice down.

Do you have a very aggressive inner voice? Do you beat up yourself a lot? Do you attack yourself a lot? Have you ever been that destructive? You can be honest and that's okay.

Or are you not destructive at all? Or are you more constructive than destructive? Do you have a very good relationship or don't you have a very good relationship? Do you have a lot of money in your bank account; do you think you are financially free? Do you have a constructive thinking of being financially free? It is not possible that you have a constructive thinking of being financially free and yet you say you are not financially independent. It just does not add up. How do I measure this? If you are above 30 and not financially free, let me tell you have been in a destructive state. Because there has to be co-ordination between your thinking and your output.

Let's take an example: today you have decided that you want to make a million dollars. What could stop you? I will give you an example: the Japanese used to carry out a form of torture – they used to make people lie down blindfolded, with water dripping on their forehead. Then they would say, 'I have a knife in my hand and I am going to cut your throat,' and they would just get a feather and just move that feather around their throat and people would die of a heart attack, thinking they were indeed using a knife.

What I am saying is that we have to be very clear that there is a co-relation in what we say to ourselves and our output. Look at your life. I guarantee you that every single problem in your life, where you have been weak is because the inner voice has been destructive. Prove me wrong…I want you to. I am not saying that I am on this mission to do something great. Of course I am not but please don't forget, even on a mission, you are going to hurt yourself a few times.

The question is, how many times are you destructive, or how many times are you constructive. So, I look around and I think to myself: if tomorrow someone kidnapped your parents and as ransom said to you that you have got two years to make it, to do whatever you have to do, to become successful and lose weight, you will do it. Because the inner voice will change from 'Can I do it?' to 'Oh my god, if I don't, this is going to happen or that is going to happen.' You don't allow your brain any choice.

Do you know what the purpose of this inner voice is? It's like a protector. It can be called the gatekeeper: anything that comes your way, it will decide if it is good for you like an over-protective parent before allowing it to go through. But sometimes, the gatekeeping is very strong because of the parenting, because of the environment you live in. 'Don't do this; you might get hurt,' or 'Don't do this or this will happen,' 'Rich people are bad,' or 'The world is a bad place.' How does people strap themselves with bombs and blow themselves up. How is that possible? There has to be information that the gatekeeper is allowing to go through.

Most people don't have any training or coaching on taming the gatekeeper. And that is the hardest part. When I see people working on content and they wonder if their content is right or the offer is right, I find it funny that they don't realise they have nothing to do with it. It has only to do with that inner voice. When you are kids, people impose stuff upon you and what if the kids believe that? The same thing happens here. If somebody performs on stage, and they are not good, if they've had a bad day, people will say it was very tough. 'It is not going to be easy. You will have to go through it.' In my mind I wonder why you would give that information to them.

When people go to trainings thinking it's going to be difficult, it's not true. Some of you will be effortless and I am telling you the only defining difference is going to be your inner voice. Ask yourself, am I worth it? The reason I tell you to make YouTube videos and do this or do that is because I want you to build that confidence in that inner voice, so that when you stand there and stand with authority, you will know that yes, people are going to pay me. Because that is the only difference and that is going to make you truly successful.

One of the clients from my Speak To a Fortune 3-month programme met me in a coffee shop, where we were discussing his programme. When I looked at him, I thought he was unsure, truly unsure of what he was going to do in his programme. That clearly showed in his body language, the faces he was making and the questions he was asking. And I was thinking, 'Will he be able to do it? Is he going to do it?' This was my inner voice.

And when we parted, we had some structure in place and he seemed as though he'd do an okay job. Obviously, his inner voice was far stronger than my inner voice because he went ahead and conducted the seminars, and pretty well at that. Even when my whole mindset was very negative about him, he was doing well because there came a point in the conversation when he went from being nervous to very sure of himself. This happened when he started talking from his inner voice and his gatekeeper had stopped interrupting.

Some of you will have very strong gatekeepers that won't allow anything to pass through, neither good thoughts and nor bad thoughts. Some of you will take time to allow things to come in, to open up; others will hold on and prevent anything from causing pain or failure.

I HONESTLY BELIEVE ARFEEN HAS GONE INTO OUR BLOODSTREAM. I KEPT IMAGINING ARFEEN, HIS HONESTY AND HIS BURNING DESIRE TO CONTRIBUTE, AND I DID SO TOO WITH THE SAME SINCERITY.

DR HIMANI SHAH TANDON, PAIN EXPERT

A GOAL IS SOMETHING YOU SET FOR YOURSELF. YOU DO NOT NEED ANYBODY TO REMIND YOU OF YOUR OWN GOALS.

2

Passion: The Key to Success

The faster you get started, the easier your journey is going to be. You don't have to be perfect. Some of you maybe into perfection a lot but the best thing to do is to get started. I am going to make it easier for you. I am going to give you a step-by-step guide on what to do for the first 90 days, so you don't have an excuse of not knowing what to do. Ok now I want you all to be very open minded. Let's try this out and see how it goes; I don't know if it works for you…if it doesn't work, it doesn't work but if it does, it'll do wonders for you. What I am going to tell you now, you can use it in your training as well. It's a very simple methodology.

Every person I coach, I use this same thing. I don't change my coaching system. I don't do one-to-one and change my system for everyone. It's the same. For me to understand you, I have to understand what you think. Because whether we like it or not, the conversation happens and most of us are not even aware of what we are thinking. We are so involved in function that we are not present in the thoughts that we have.

The greatest place to be in is the present. There's no point being in the past and there's no point really in being in the future because you don't know what's going to happen. But it's better to know where you stand right now. I'll stand on the stage and I'll think about myself…the first question that I ask myself is, 'What do I believe about who I am? Will I ever discover that in totality? Probably not?'

But let's get to a point where you can discover who I am from the perspective of a speaker, trainer coach, and consultant at least. Now I am going to teach you and coach you as well. Anything that you have to do in life ever, you have got to start as if the situation is today. Because you can't assume. You wouldn't know what's going on in somebody else's head. We have to assume by understanding where we are right now.

The only way to create change is to be aware. Awareness gives you a perspective about where you stand. Now whether you are right or wrong about it, I don't know, but we'll work on that factor. I just want you to put yourselves in a situation where you are an expert, speaker or coach – whatever you want to call yourself. And when I make the following statements, and I want you to imagine what comes to your mind, don't try to be positive, just think normally. And you can apply this to any programme. Don't think too much about it; just list things down. There is no right or wrong answer.

Exercise

1. For me to become a great speaker, expert or coach I must… (Do what)
2. I believe the following 3 things about me must change… (List those things)
3. My 2 greatest fears of doing this kind of work are… (List them)
4. The reason why I can't charge so and so amount of rupees for my programme is… (Choose any appropriate figure for yourself, minimum 10 lacs.)
5. As I go on stage, this is what I am thinking… (List those things) if you have not been on stage, imagine you are about to.
6. My greatest fear as a speaker, expert or coach is…
7. For me to be the best, I must believe what about myself?

8. When people come up to me and tell me I am good, this is what I think about me. (List your thoughts)
9. For me to make a great transformation for somebody, I must believe______about me. (Any 3 things about you)
10. For me to be truly successful, I must speak…? (e.g., the truth, speak out…)
11. Hiding in the back, being silent or quiet will do what for my future?

A RARE COMBINATION OF A PERSON WHO IS INSPIRING MILLIONS THROUGH HIS WORK, AS WELL AS A GEM OF A HUMAN BEING, WHICH IS RARE TO COME BY. YOU ARE THE RIGHT DEFINITION OF A LEADER WHO KNOWS HOW TO NURTURE OTHER LEADERS.

RAVNEET SINGH, BODY & MIND EXPERT

**DARE TO DREAM.
ONLY THEN CAN IT BE
REALISED AND ACHIEVED.**

3

What's Your Story?

You all may come across a situation wherein, you may say I want to talk confidently, but what you are concerned about is that you don't want to look bad in front of people. I will tell you one more thing about being a speaker, expert or coach or consultant – if you are not going to look bad; you will never do well.

If you look at my seminars, you might have noticed that in my seminar I talk about my personal stories, I am very open in my programmes. You might say that I am being very transparent, but I only talk about stuff that I have dealt with. I don't talk about my ongoing issues. But the fact that I don't worry about what you might think of me, makes my programme more powerful and effective.

The most powerful word that I would like to teach you and we should add it in the course is 'vulnerability'. Because when you are vulnerable, it makes you powerful. It makes you not scared of what people think of you, or of people judging you. What if I look bad, what if I say something wrong, what if I have to prepare before I call people about what I will say to them. This ability is power. The more vulnerable you are, the more powerful you become in front of everyone.

If you think you are too young to earn a lot of money and you are in the phase of getting experience, let me tell you Mark Zuckerberg is very young and he is earning a lot, so do you mean to say he should not be earning so much. So, this is myth or you can say it's just an excuse. If you are saying that you don't deserve to charge 10 lacs just because you think you are not giving enough value to the person, that means you are saying you are not good enough.

Let me give you my own example: when I started selling this seminar, I started it at 3 lacs a year and I used to find it really difficult to sell it and I used to think to myself that, 'Am I not worth this? Because I know my seminar and I love it!' But then I realised I was selling it for a lesser price. So, one day while going to my seminar, I decided to sell it for a higher price and I asked my team to change all the offers and I went on stage and I sold it for 7 lacs and I got more subscriptions. Selling became easy because I realised my worth and I was selling it for a much lesser price. Now, I have raised it to 9 lacs and soon I shall increase it even more. I should know what I am worth. And my knowledge makes me feel valuable. The code that you have, is going to be with you, and it has nothing to do with content.

You should have a mindset that you can provide value worth the cost of your programme. If it is somebody famous like Dhoni, Sachin Tendulkar, Mukesh Ambani, Amitabh Bachchan, do you believe that you can meet them and coach them? If I had to meet Mukesh Ambani today, and coach him and tell him what to do, I would have no problem in telling him what to do. Hrithik Roshan goes in a speaking engagement, he goes for one hour and he charges 1 Cr. Maybe Shah Rukh Khan is charging something similar or maybe more than this. Now the question is why people are paying them this 1 Cr.

My point is…why are these people charging so much of money?

And why do people pay them?

The reason is these people project value. Cricketers and sports people are usually more famous than others celebrities. Is it because of skill? Some are famous for their personalities as well. The only thing that matters is your current code about yourself? When you meet a person one-to-one, in my mind for example, I believe whenever I meet someone, he will walk away with a transformation and I don't know any better. So, if I am in my mindset and if I meet you, the transformation has to happen.

You can put together a programme today and sell it for 5-10 lacs right away even if you are very new to this. If you think: 'How can I coach people if I am not sorted in my life,' then let me tell you one more thing, your life is never going to be perfect. I had relationship crisis with my wife in my early days, and I used to wonder how I am going to coach people about relationships when I haven't got mine in order. But then that also motivated me to turn around my perspective to at least try to find a way out of my own relationship.

I also faced a financial crisis and again I found the same issue of how I will coach people if I am not stable myself. So, you have to find a solution and you have to say it to yourself: 'My vulnerabilities are my power.' How do you decide if someone values you or not? You can't, right?

Do you know Tony Robbins? When I met him, he told me, 'You have the key to everybody's front door,' and I said, 'What do you mean?' To which he said, 'Everybody you know on this planet has something that they need to fix. Every human being on earth, be it the King of Saudi Arabia or Donald Trump, the King of Dubai, Mr. Narendra Modi or all the leaders of the world, all the business owners, all the famous people and all of these have something that they need to fix.'

And if you have the solution for that, they would hold you in high value. So, I have coached at least 4 billionaires and I am nowhere close to being a billionaire. So, why would they come to me? I know I can coach any human on this planet and I will produce value. If you have something of value, the only thing that can stop you here is your code. A doubt even the size of a mustard seed is not allowed.

I acted in one movie and I can guarantee you that if I acted in two more movies, I would succeed and a lot many people would know me then. I am confident because that's my code and I can't do any better. Why not charge Rs 10 lacs for your programme for a period of 1 year. If you do 10 such programmes in a year, you would be earning 1 Cr. a year. What can be your doubt? The doubt is 'Oh my God, should I ask?' Maybe the doubt is pressure of sales if you charge more. And that happens because we start anticipating reaching our target sales. What should be done is, at least this is what I do, whenever I am taking seminars, not for once in my mind am I thinking of:'I better close 25 people or 50 people.'

I think I am going to go out there and produce the best of what I can and that's what my code asks me to do. And the byproduct of this will be the result. When I do well, people will see me, and I will do better next time. But when you go without expectations in your mind, you will always produce results. Your system should be strong, so, despite your mood, your code should work for you. What most speakers do is they learn some content and come on stage to vomit it out verbally with the help of PowerPoint presentations. And to be different from them, you need to sort your code and start having a mindset about an outstanding speaker, coach, expert or consultant.

To have a perfect code to work for you, you have got to be very confident and fearless. You have to create a space where you believe you can charge any amount of money and all the people that hang around this circle will come to you. It is like you meet a person and they introduce you to their friends and then these friends will further introduce you to their friends and the circle continues. Don't think what your audience will think. Believe that you can do it.

Let's take the example of an art auction. People bid on an art piece and the price of an art piece goes higher. Human beings tend to think when the price is high, the value that they will get would also be higher.

This is human mentality, when the price is high, they feel the value that they will get would also be higher. When you buy a branded perfume, what do you pay for? The perfume costs nothing; you pay for the bottle and the label on it. The bottle and the packaging are what people get attracted to. Of course, the perfume has to be good as well. All you need to do is believe in yourself that you can provide a value and then you can charge for any amount of money effortlessly. The rule is you never discuss your business with people; the reason is not that they would be negative but not everybody would understand.

For example, until recently, my mother used to tell me, 'Why you don't get yourself a decent job?' You have to know that you can deliver that transformation. In your mind, you need to project that you are a person of a particular value, before you project that outside. My code is that people will pay. People always pay. Why will they not pay? If I am offering you something that I know can have a radical transformation. I have to know that the transformation is real.

What I am delivering will produce a result eventually. I know what I am producing and if I believe that, and I believe in my work and in what I am saying, I can charge you. What I don't do is: 'That guy has charged this much or this guy has charged this much.' I have no idea of what my competitor is charging.

In my business plan, if you ask me who is my competition, I will say, 'Nobody.' I am sure they are out there, but I am not really interested in knowing what they are doing. I have a business, I want to charge, and I need to deliver, so, I believe I need to be paid a certain amount for this. I have always added more value to the programme, so, I know now. Over a period of time, I am going to add more value and people will pay for that.

What do we do to become effortless? What do we do so that whenever you want to do something, you don't have to put a lot of effort in it? I don't believe in effort. I think effort should happen as a byproduct of your thoughts. So, let's take an example: Michael Jackson once said in his interview upon being asked that how long did he take to write 'Billie Jean' (his song) and he said, 'I did not write the song, the song wrote me,' which means it just comes.

Have you ever experienced not thinking of any idea and it just popped up and you say, 'Wow! This was really good.' Happens with me all the time, many times I say many things in my seminars and I say to myself, 'Wow! This is amazing and I hope I don't forget these.' And then when someone asks you what you said, you can't remember, because things happen effortlessly. And the reason why this happens is because of whom you believe you are, what your identity, your code is.

Let's take a situation: a plane has crash into a building and you are nearby. And you can hear people crying and the plane is on fire and there are these huge flames coming out and there are huge chances if you go near you might get burnt and also a chance that you might save somebody. Now these flames are really powerful and there is a possibility of an explosion happening. You don't know if you are going to survive.

Now think very carefully and ask yourself a question, what would a person who is terrified, do? Might run the other way, because his code is 'I am terrified.' What would Captain America do? He would go in, would he have any doubts? What would the Incredible Hulk do? He wouldn't go in…he would smash his way through. What would Superman do?

He would zoom in pick up and get out. Would he walk in? No, because he is coded to be super.

When you come into a situation in your life, your code kicks in and then you start deciding how you are going to act upon it. So, I come into a situation here, I have a course to do, I have to now decide subconsciously who I am and behave accordingly. So, if you could, write down some power codes and ask some power questions; that will help you redefine your codes a little bit.

I will tell you how to do that. So, if you have children and you are working and when you come back tired, your child wants to play with you, but your code could be: 'Leave me alone, I have had a bad day.' Now this is not a very constructive code for a child. What should the code be? 'I always give time to my children, no matter what': suppose that was your code that day and when you came home from a really tired day and your kids come running to you, what will you do? Will you say,'No, I am not in the mood today?' No, because your code doesn't allow that. If your children were in trouble, would you help them? You would, right? No matter what. And why is that so? Because it is your code.

What I am saying is that what if we could define a set of codes? What are my codes? Everything happens for a reason and that reason serves me which means if I go through an adverse situation or if I am going through a difficult time, what would be my natural reaction to that. I am not going to say I was OK. I am going to know in the back of my mind that this served me. And what will I look for in that problem? What if I say that everything always happens to me? When I am in a bad situation, what am I going to do? What am I going to look for? Will I be able to see anything good? No, because your brain will delete and distort information that is not relevant to the code you have.

You may say, 'Oh my God, Arfeen, that's so systematic, I don't want to live like that.' But you already have a code. There is a code that is undecided for you. Some of you have the code that when you come on the stage, you are not going to be loud and you are going to be very quiet and that's the code that you have got. Some of you would meet new people for the first time and you may not be the first one to go up and say hello to them. Because you might be thinking, 'I better not talk or they may not converse with me or talk to me.' That's the code you have developed.

Some people might say, 'I am not doing a particular thing because I am not allowed or people in my family don't want me to do this because they think I am going to fail in it.' I don't know if that's true or not. Maybe that's your reason to not want to take action. I won't say excuse because some people will sabotage themselves by putting impediments around them that would prevent them from taking action. Some people will never take risks in life and they tell people it's because they don't want to get hurt. My point to you is that your code will define the quality of everything that you ever do in your life. And you already have your code.

Do you have a code?

Do you have a money management system? The fact is you do have a money management system. Now it may be not be decided by you but when the money comes in, you do something with it, right? So, even if you think you don't have a code, you do have a code. A speaker code, a transformational code, a code that you live by. If I told you for a seminar the amount of preparation that I do is a few pointers and when do I do it? I do it on the day of the seminar taking almost 7-10 mins. Now can I do a full day's programme with content that I know is going to be effective without having to do preparation for it? How? Because I know I can. It's in my gut, it's in my brain and I know it's going to happen.

Why should it not happen? It would be unnatural for me not to be able to do this. Because this is a code.

Do you have difficulties talking to someone new? That is definitely not a good code. I used to make many notes and one fine day, I realised that whatever I am doing are my notes and then I had my PowerPoint. I started using PowerPoint and then a day came when I realised, I know my subject and I should be able to do it. It can so happen that you start feeling that all problems come to you. But remember, you can either be part of the problem or you can be part of the solution and that depends on your code!

Have you heard of Will Smith? Do you know everything that Will Smith does works? Have you ever heard him speak? The way this guy speaks, you know everything this guy will do has to work because his thinking process and his coding is unreal and it is fabulous. So, if you are earning Rs 50, 000 a month and working for 11-12 hours then you are earning just Rs 135 in an hour and that comes to $2 an hour. And India is a country where you can earn at least $50 i an hour, in the profession that we are in. Some of you may wonder how that is possible for you. But when you read my manual and see the first page, it will give you a description of exactly what is a 1 million-dollar opportunity. There is always a belief issue and that's the reason I have added this topic to this book. The only question I am going to leave you with is why can't you charge more? If you could run a course for a year or 6 months or 1 month, whatever you are doing then, why can't you charge more? I am not telling you to charge an X amount of money…I am saying why can't you?

Now let's imagine you are going to take a seminar and you will be charging Rs 1 lac for it, so, what is your code going to be? List down 10 codes that you need for this seminar. These codes should have a compelling language. For example, you can't say I will be happy as a code. Use a language, when you stand on the stage and you have to say those codes to you, it should give you a certain feeling in your body. For example, words like 'unstoppable', it would give you a vibe in your body. When you are writing your codes, don't forget negative codes are as powerful as positive codes. We always emphasise on why this always happen, why this hell always break loose on me. That's a code, right? You need to use a language that is compelling. Next, you need to list down 20 questions that would lead to that code.

Let me explain this: if I say I want to be a contributor, the question I would ask is: 'What can I do so people walk out with some kind of transformation?' If I ask that question, what will it make me into? A great contributor! So what do questions do for you? Questions give you focus. 'How can I become rich? What 3 things can I do now to become rich?' Does the second question make me more focused? Yes, the quality of questions will determine the quality of your life. When you go on stage and you are nervous, the question you are asking could be: 'What if they laugh at me? What if I forget my lines? What if I forget my content?' Those questions will make you have a code of insecurity or nervousness.

If you are going for an audition and you look around and see 10 more people there and you walk in and think: 'Oh my God, the other person looks better than me or the other person is more confident than me,' the code starts kicking into negativity. But if you are in that surrounding, what could you ask yourself to make you bring out the code of unstoppable? Because I always compete against myself. Your code can be a simple statement. I can say to myself, 'What can I do now to make me even more competitive? What can I do now that will make me grow as a person?'

I am just asking you because when you go on stage, the first thing that will happen is, to get into state. Of course, your body language should be good, but the quality of your questions will determine how or what code is coming in. If I ask a whole bunch of really good powerful questions, it will make you feel unstoppable and the word should be 'unstoppable'.

If a person is shy to talk to people they don't know, what should be their code be? It can be…if I walk into an event, I will be the first one to talk to people or I am a great contributor. What would such a person need to ask themselves in order to go and talk to people? They could say, 'What can I do now to add value to a person's life?' That might encourage the person to go and talk to others. The quality of questions will determine the quality of your thinking. You don't have to be a great speaker, trainer, coach all the time.

Let's take an example of Superman and Clark Kent… they are not the same people, so what can Superman's code be? 'To save people, fly faster than the speed of light, nothing can stop me, I am bulletproof, always go for higher heights,' and what will be Clark Kent's code? Studious, quite, nervous. His code is somewhere different from Superman's.

When Superman wants to become Superman, what does he do? He breaks through the old code or switches codes. Does that mean Clark has to be Superman all the time? No, so when does Superman become Super? When he needs to... Super heroes are good metaphors, they are saying: 'You don't have to be a speaker, trainer, coach all the time but when you come into the zone where you have to be a speaker or trainer, you need to show your uniform.' What is Superman's 'S'? It's his code. It's his identity: 'When I am wearing this Superman outfit, I must become powerful.'

So, when you come on to the stage or you are doing a one-to-one or you are doing group-coaching or you are writing your book, what code should kick in? Your code has to kick in, no time for excuses, no time for negativity, and no time for bullshit. It is going to be that code and that's what

I am trying to help you discover. The reason why we love superheroes – they all have codes.

The Incredible Hulk, what is his code? Smash! He grows. What colour is he? Green. When is he angry? He says his secret is that he is always angry. But does he show his anger all the time? OK and what is his other code as a person? What is he like? Very mild, kind of a quiet, lonely guy, walks around by himself. Let's talk about Batman, what is his code? He is dark, he hides in a cave, he is secret and no one knows him.

What is your code? If you are a mother, you have a mother code or if you are a father, you have a father code and if you are a wife, you have a wife code. Did you exactly sit down and make it? No, but it is developed and it is there. Your kids should speak to you in a certain way and that's your code. They should be home by 7 and that's your code. There should be certain things that are your code.

What I am saying is instead of going with the flow, why not write your own 10 Commandments. Codes will get you into your state, which is your relationship activity, and your state will produce thoughts, and your thoughts will produce actions and behaviors and results. Whatever preparations you are in, whatever job title you are in, whatever relationship you are in, write your codes out and you will be shocked, what happens. This is the simplest form of coaching in the history of the world; as far as I am concerned, this is what I use. This is how people get rid of any behaviour.

Suppose you have a wife code, you could look at your current code and list things as destructive and constructive and change all destructive codes into constructive ones. Do you go to a social environment and you are comfortable talking to the people you don't know? Say you are in a coffee shop; can you strike up a conversation every time? That's your code.

What if you met say M.S. Dhoni, the cricketer standing in a hotel lobby and you walked in, would you be able to go up to him and not say 'Hello Sir, how are you?' but say, 'Hey buddy, long time no see?' Again that's a code issue. Why would you not say that to him?

I met M.S. Dhoni at Taj Lands' End, and I tapped him and said, 'Hey, how are you doing? I am Arfeen,' and I said, 'You are a great cricketer but you know what, you should talk to me, I can really make a difference in your life.' Can you imagine that? And he is probably looking at me thinking I don't know what's going on. But he is not going to forget me; I was not rude at all. He asked me, 'What do you do?' and I said, 'I am a performance speaker coach,' and he said, 'Yes, I know about performance coach and lots of cricketers have them now.' I gave him my card, and of course he did not give me his card. But the point is would you be able to do so? Again that is a code issue. Everybody you ever meet in your proximity is a potential person who needs your help, but if your code stops you... It's all about the code.

Examples of Strong Codes

1. My vision is bigger than the moment.
2. I set a benchmark every single time.
3. Transformation is easy for me to create.
4. I am the creator of powerful experiences.
5. My passion and conviction will shine through.
6. I focus on my values and success is guaranteed.
7. Success is the only option.
8. I am in my most empowering state today.
9. I am unstoppable, powerful and confident.
10 My system gives results effortlessly, every single time.

If you are about to present something of high value and with this belief, how would you feel about that? Now I want you to imagine that you are walking into a room and now as you are walking into this room, you listen to sound of 1000's of people calling out your name. And as you are walking, you can feel your heart beating and as you walk, you think about all those people that you are going to help change life or transform. And as you are walking you start telling yourself: 'My vision is far bigger than this moment' and as you say that, how does it make you feel? And as you take another step, you start telling yourself: 'I set a benchmark every single time I possibly can' and as you say this, you can feel your body, your heart, your energy inside of you. And you can hear the sound of those people walking, shouting and screaming your name. And you think that this is your moment as you think about what you are going to do; you realise a transformation is so easy. If you are ready to transform your life and do what you love, you need to check out my Speak To a Fortune 3-month programme.

How to Build Your Credibility

Everyone has got this concept in their mind, that if I do my first seminar, I am successful. That is not true at all, because anyone can do a seminar. That's not difficult to do. If you are able to build your credibility, about who you are, people will respect you more.

For example, whom would you listen to more…somebody who has written three books, or someone who has a blog, or someone who has a YouTube channel, or someone who has written many books on a subject. Obviously, someone who has written many books on a subject. If you prove your credibility, people start seeing you as an expert. And if they don't see you as an expert, they are not going to pay you the money.

The people who get paid the most money are the people who are experts in what they do. Look at doctors – you have a general practitioner and you have a neuro specialist. Who gets paid more?

A neuro specialist, right?

And why he is paid more is because of his specialisation. Now I am going to say this today and I know I will have to repeat it again and again. People say, 'Why will people pay me? Arfeen for you it is very easy. 'Let me tell you it is not easy for me.

If I am doing a seminar today, and 90% of the audience is brand new. If you are doing a seminar today, 90% of your audience is brand new too, they don't know you and they don't know me. Why should they buy from me and not from you? Give me a logic in that, because most people who come to the event are brand new. They don't know me, why are they going to buy for me. It can either be that my conviction shows more. It has nothing to do with the way you are as a speaker, I don't believe that.

It could do with the presentation, the projection; when you read about me and you read my profile and read what I have done and that might say larger-than-life, that's important. Why would they spend 9 lakhs with me and in some cases not spend 9 lakhs with you. But I know I can charge that comfortably, effortlessly and others may have difficulty doing that. Someone may say, 'Arfeen, you have got more experience,' and I say, 'That has got nothing to do with it. In my Speak To a Fortune 3-month programme, I help my participants have their first seminar, and we help them arrange everything.'

What can it be? Someone like you can decide now to start with a new programme and charge 9 lakhs from day 1. Why can I do it and not you? It has got all to do with how you put together this whole jigsaw puzzle. The good thing is, in this day and age, to publish yourself is really easy to do.

Would you not like to have your own TV show? Do you know what the cost to host a TV show is? There is production cost, there is finding a channel and there is lot more. But all this is not true; having a TV show is free. You can have a TV show right now. The question is how?

Facebook live is your answer. What you can do is, you can set up your room with the background reading 'The Arfeen Khan Show' and announce it say every Tuesday 7 p.m. You can do a professional setup if you want, you can put two cameras and actually have a really high-end digital TV show live on Facebook and build your audience over a period of time. How much does this cost you? Zero. And who is your audience? There are two billion people on Facebook right now; that's insane. And it costs you nothing.

You can actually have a two-camera setup, edit it, and do a professional set-up. I can do a Facebook live in the middle of my seminar, I just have to login into Facebook and everybody can see my seminar and it would cost me nothing because Facebook does not charge me. No restriction on length and you can do Facebook live for an entire day as far as I know. Now imagine over a period of time you build up a TV show, you announce it and slowly you have 5 people come in, your content is very good then you have 10 people coming and then 50, 100 and then maybe a 1000 and then you would start engaging them and start presenting your show. Today, all this is very easy.

You can publish your book yourself; you don't need a publisher anymore. You can write a book, you can get an ISBN number and then you can put it on Amazon, Flipkart and you are published. Can you imagine how cool that is; you can do a podcast if you want to where you can do a weekly programme and put it on Apple or put it on any podcast and again, it costs you nothing. You could make an audio series online and what would that cost you? Nothing. Most of the softwares are free.

You can publish yourself today better than anyone in history could and I mean anyone. In the past, how difficult was it for you to make a YouTube video recording? Today, everyone has a camera in their hands. And now with your new cameras, the quality of the pictures is absolutely out of this world. They are just amazing so, you can even do that. There is so much to do, the whole world can see you today and it will cost you almost nothing. If I were to do a survey right now of all the people that have been in my Speak To a Fortune programme for six months or more, I can guarantee you that 90% of them haven't done even a 10% of what they are being told.

Now I am not going to take responsibility or ownership of that, but I can tell you that whatever is given to you, if you are not making good use of it, then I can't make you do that. And I am also telling you that all this is very important for your entire life. So you have to define your programme, you might develop a system through research, but you need to explain what this system does. For example, if I eat Vitamin C, it will help me improve my immune system.

Similarly, when I do your programme, what is it going to do for me? After defining your programme and how it would help me, you need to prove this to me. I will need actual proof that you have the right to teach me this. I will explain what my point here exactly is: when I come on the stage and speak on my programme, I am sure of my programme, and I believe I have the right to teach it and I can prove it to you as well. I can give you actual evidence that what I am teaching you, I do it myself and the evidence happens when you come to my seminar. We are in a room, I do a presentation, I upsell and people buy.

I am asking you to prove that you are a master or expert in what you say you are going to do in your programme. It can be a tangible or a non-tangible proof. This is a hard part and this is where you will start bashing yourself up. I come up to you and say I am a doctor; I am sitting at my house and I say, 'You know what, I can operate on you,' and now if you don't know me, would you like to know where I work, would you like to get some proof on what kind of doctor I am or would you just say to me, 'No problem, do the surgery? So, the point here is if you are offering a solution, I want proof. And you have to give a proof that you are allowed to do this.

You may have the world's best system designed but if you come on stage and say, 'I can help anyone get any result', in my mind as an audience what am I thinking at that moment is: 'What's the proof?' I can say I can help any person, any company perform their best, but show me the proof, because when you are going to establish your story well, people will pay you whatever you want.

When you buy a book, what is the first place you look at? The back cover? When you go on Amazon to buy a book, what do you check? Reviews? Because you want to know what people are saying about the book; you are looking for proof that the book is good. Or if somebody came up to you saying that this book is amazing, that is a proof enough; if you trust that person you will go and buy that book the very next day.

'Programme' as a term is way too broad. The more outcomes you have, the more proofs you will require and the more proof you need, the harder you will have to work. What you have to remember here is that you have to go narrow. You have to become an expert in one thing. Because if you specialise in one thing, you can start building massive evidence around it.

I met somebody, who teaches people how to manage anger. 'What else can you do?' And he said, 'The people who cannot sleep at night; I can help them do so. It's a huge problem worldwide and I thought what if I became an expert in helping people go to sleep – that's a huge market.' He will have to prove what he could do around that; how do you prove that people are going to sleep – testimonials or his own story…there can be a 100 ways to do it. But because he has narrowed it down, he can become known in India as the man who puts people to sleep. Besides, he can do 10 other things, he is really good with other topics as well. Every time, I meet him he is coming out with a new topic.

The first started with him measuring your pulse and he can tell you what your body diagnoses is, then he did anger management, then he went on to relationship, then he went on to emotional management and there are many things. But the problem is if he does all of them, he has to prove all of them. And you have to become an expert in one. It doesn't mean in the future you can't have multiple expertise but it has got to start with one.

If you had to pick on one thing that you think you can do, then what do you think it can be? What can you do every single time? And of course, you have to back it up with proof. When we ask for proof the natural thing that people do is they start giving content. While it is very natural for people to do that, imagine me coming to you and saying 'I believe' and you would probably say, 'OK. Where is your proof?' despite my shouting again, 'I still believe'. Instead if I gave you proof, it makes me credible, it makes you viable.

If you don't become an expert in one thing or you don't build your story around it, you have to keep building your story over and over again till that story becomes so big that people talk about it. A critical difference between trainers and transformational experts is that the former cannot provide proof. Trainers make no money, you can make a lac or maybe two lacs if you are lucky but transformational experts make a fortune.

Let's take an example: in the past you have helped 50 women start their business. You have helped them get clarity, so now how are you going to build a story around this. These women are married and have children and now they are getting back to business. So, what can be the product ideas?

Some ideas can be as under:

1. You could go to 20 women who are married, have children and have started from scratch and have built great businesses, and interview them. Maybe you can ask them about their secret.
2. You could write a book on those 20 women and their experiences and maybe name it 'India's most successful housewife' or 'From housewife to millionaire'.
3. You can do a Facebook live and interview women. Women who want to be successful, women who are struggling and thinking they have worked before, have had children and now that the kids have grown up, what should they do. These women need guidance.
4. You could get banks to help these women; you can get other expert women building businesses and interview them, do blogs and videos with them.
5. You could write articles in women's magazines.
6. You could even start a magazine maybe by the name *Let's Go, Women.*
7. You could make an audio series or a DVD kit that you can give away or sell at a very low price maybe named 'Get started'

The point is you can build up an entire story just around one field that we have talked about. People have to relate to you and they relate to you based on their story. People only buy from people who understand each other. You come to my programme and you purchase it because there is something in my programme where you and I clicked. And you felt that I had something that you want, or you might have thought that I could understand your problem. There can be no other reason. It cannot be because you like me or something like that, because nobody is going to spend that kind of money just because they like me. We clicked and that was something.

Similarly, your story has to be defined. And if your story is not defined, you will do what I did. You will create a fantastic product. I made a product called 'Personal Mastery' which was a 27-CD programme; it was fantastic, but I could sell only 5000 copies of that CD whereas I should have actually sold 500,000 copies of this CD set. But why could I not do so? Because for whom was this product? It was for everyone. For me selling the programme is the hardest part, the rest of the programme is very easy.

When you choose a subject, your future study is assured because you need to study advance techniques on the same subject, you will research on the same subject, and you will meet people about the same subject. Over time you build up the collateral, you build up all this content. When you say this man has got over 30 years of experience in one specific field, that's what gives credibility.

Your outcome will affect lots of areas, but for what will you be known? So the question you need to ask is: 'What do I want to be known for? If by now, you are wondering, 'How am I going to prove anything?' it is normal. Don't panic. If you are not sure about your subject, don't worry, you have an opportunity to get the Speak To a Fortune programme at a special price; just go to speaktofortune.com/letter.

Many people ask me this question: 'How long did it take for you to start doing well?' I took 10 years to get things in order. And I will make you do this in 6 months to a year. It's a big shortcut and even now, the only thing I am trying to do is build up a story. Let me tell you the method that I believe works every single time. And this is furnishes the real proof of what you believe in.

Do you know Jim Rohn? He is considered the grandfather of the Self-Help movement. He is my favourite; he passed away a few years ago. Jim Rohn is an amazing speaker, he is fabulous. Tony Robbins used to work for Jim Rohn. You might know Tony Robbins, Zig Ziglar, Brian Tracy, Les Brown, and Robert Kiyosaki .

Who taught Jim Rohn to speak? Where did he get his content from? Nobody! He is an untrained speaker. Untrained means nobody taught him how to stand on a stage or talk to people. And who taught Tony Robbins to speak? He did work for Jim Rohn, but not as a speaker' he used to sell tickets for him. Again, nobody taught Tony Robbins to be a speaker; he learnt himself. Who taught Zig Ziglar, Brian Tracy, Les Brown, and Robert Kiyosaki to speak? As far as I know, nobody taught them. Have you heard Jim Rohn speak? His subject is Wisdom and Common Sense. Where does he get his knowledge from? From his own experience. Of all the knowledge that he gives, how much comes from outside or external sources? Hardly anything. I can't remember even a single incident that he spoke about covering anything he has ever learnt from anywhere else.

Have you heard Tony Robbins speak? Where does he get his knowledge from? Almost 90% of his content is from his own experience.

Les Brown has his experiences from his own challenges. He might have about 30% external content. Brian Tracy, again his own experiences; Robert Kiyosaki doesn't have his own content; somebody else writes for him as far as I know. But of all the superstars out there, how many have been trained to speak? None!

Jim Rohn, would you say he is real and authentic? He is really authentic; when you listen to him, it is just awesome. Tony Robbins, is he authentic? Les Brown, does he come under authentic? Absolutely. Zig Ziglar, does he come under authentic? Now why are they all authentic? It's because it is their story and it is coming from within.

Most trainers, speakers and coaches are told to mug up a subject and deliver it; that doesn't work. Everyone has a story; some have a dramatic story. Some have small stories. You have a story that goes up and down and you have gone through your challenges; you come out of these challenges and again you go through them and come out of them. And your story will make people connect with you because they know you mean what you say and you say what you mean. So, if I pick up content from Daniel Goleman, I learn it and I present it to you, I can never get emotional about Daniel Goleman's content. Or even if I try, I can never really get the feel of that content.

A few years back, I went to Camp America – it is a chance for you to go on a camp, and help children as a counsellor. So, they paid for my flight. I was a student, and I went there for six weeks, taking care of children. It was great fun in the United States. After camp, they gave you time to travel. So I went to New York to a friend and she said to me, 'Why you don't leave the baggage at my house and when you fly back, pick it up and go home?'

I went to her place and I met her father and he asked me, 'When will you be back?'

I said, 'I will be back on Friday.'

He asked, 'What time?'

I said, 'I will be back by 4 o'clock.'

On Friday, I reached her place at 5 o'clock. I knocked on the door and her dad opened it.

I said, 'Hi, can I have my bags?'

He said, 'No.'

I asked, 'Why?'

'You had said you would come back by 4 o'clock.'

And I replied, 'It is New York and people get late.'

He said in a harsh tone, 'I am never late and 4 o'clock means 4 o'clock, so you cannot get your bags.'

I said, 'I have my flight tonight.'

He said, 'That's not my problem. Tough luck!'

I was confused about what to do. I had no money. I just had $5-$10 in my pocket. I could not stay in a hotel. What could I do now.

I told him in a low tone, 'I have no money.'

But with aggression he said, 'Tough luck; you say 4 o'clock, so 4 o'clock.'

So I said, 'Ok, when can I come back.'

He said, 'Monday.'

I said, 'I can't come back on Monday; I got nowhere to sleep.'

All he said was, 'Tough luck!'

I went away and I was in New York City and I had nowhere to stay. Now you can go to a cockroach-infested motel or hostel there; that costs almost nothing. But I couldn't stay there because I had only $10 in my pocket and I could not afford even that. I had no money; I was broke.

So I slept in Times Square for two nights in New York, terrified, because this idiot wouldn't give my luggage. I went back on Monday and was I late? I could not afford to be late because this guy would not give me my luggage for a month. I can never forget that episode.

I could create a programme on time management based on this, proof that this is what I have gone through. I can also write a book, 'How I learnt to manage my time by sleeping on the streets of New York.' I could do a video series and find all the other people who have been through similar experiences and tell them how it changed their life. Just with that alone, we could make a transformation. One incident of your life can make you a million dollars a year from a business perspective.

What is your story? What are you trying to get out there? What are you trying to build? Because that's what it is about. You have to build the packaging and people don't do that. You know your story, you know your content, so you don't really have to prepare for it; it is going to be effortless for you. You don't have to make an effort to remember. As I am talking to you, the New York story just came up. Just because it is part of my story, it popped up. Even you might have gone through this, you are talking and suddenly great ideas pop up.

I guarantee most of them are your stories, all things that you experienced around you. And that's where people fail, this is the difference between a trainer who makes no money and someone who becomes a transformational expert and makes a fortune. I am talking about decent money. But transformational experts make money and you know what you have got to transform – the simplest or the easiest things that you can possibly find.

What I believe is we have got to establish credibility.

There are two ways of doing this:

1: You can decide on what pain you want to fix. You can decide what it is in which you want to become an expert.
2: You can decide to discover your pain from your story.

Let's take an example; I want to create a programme on 'Mr. Right'; what pain am I trying to fix? Who is my potential client? Not women! That's a too broad an audience; I can say women who are looking for a relationship, someone who has been in a number of bad relationships, who is in the age group of 23-35. So, what story can I build around this?

If this is to be created by a female author, she can write a book about how she got her Mr. Right. I can do articles in newspapers. What kind of articles could these be:

- 10 biggest mistakes women make while finding their Mr. Right.
- A book named *I Got Mr. Right.*
- Indirect promotion by getting mentioned in someone else's book.
- A talk show on 'Where to Find Mr. Right.'

Dating is huge in India now and it is not going away. I can build a whole industry around this. We can do a CD programme, we can do software, we can do a box, a pamphlet, an action guide, and we can do an audio or a video.

Your story is going to define your income.

My mother-in-law was also a participant in my Speak To a Fortune 3-month programme.

She joined but she was confused about what she could talk about, but I knew she had amazing stories to tell. I know that for her age, she definitely looks younger. I have seen her looking older and fat and then coming back to becoming slimmer and also looking younger than her age. I don't know what she does, but she does something. There has got to be a system that she has.

I know that after 40, many women go through a very difficult phase in their life, because when a man gets older it doesn't really matter. Wrinkles make a man look mature but many women live under the pressure of beauty magazines and what they watch on TV – that you have to remain young forever. So many people are going through cosmetic surgery, Botox fixes and more now. But my mother-in-law must have a system as she doesn't age. Instead, she looks younger.

What if she could help women in certain age groups to remain young? That's a huge market place. But for her to do that, her own story is not enough. People can say, 'You are lucky or you are born young.' But what if she decided to write a book, what if she decided to go and interview some of the famous women on earth like Hema Malini, Rekha, Simi Garewal, Dimple Kapadia or whoever else she or the world deems beautiful. And just go meet these people and ask them not normal questions like what is your diet, but questions on how they think…

- What happens in their mind for them to remain young?
- What is their secret?
- What makes them look the way they look?

She can do a whole series of books or a series of videos, interviews with these people, put a software together on what to do on a daily basis. she does meditation; she can put together a plan on how to do it; what exercise to do for which area and put together an entire programme with evidence that you can remain young forever.

It's a mental game; if you do not know how old you are, how would you know if it's time to get old? The reason most married people get older quicker is because they see their kids grow up. They think my kid is 18, my god I am getting old. I have seen people who remain young despite having older kids because they practice being younger in their mind as their kids get older.

We can take that one subject – how to remain young – because across the world, the number or beauty parlours and skin clinics that are popping up is unreal and the large number of people who are going there are women as well men – everybody wants to remain young. As you put together a youth programme, and you make it credible, nothing can prevent you from asking for money because you believe you have the right to ask for it, and what gives you that credibility is the content built around your story. I have helped so many of my participants find their subject, and have helped them come up with crazy ideas to build their credibility!

There are so many things that you can do.

For example, your profile. So, your profile is your story. When you meet people and they ask you to introduce yourself, there has to be a story attached to it. Because if I say, 'Ladies and gentleman for the past 10 years I have done absolutely nothing in my life and now I am going to teach you how to make a fortune', you would ask me to get lost! You can either define the topic or subject that you want to teach and build a story around it or we find out from your story what you should be teaching.

If you say, for instance,'I know how to help people get clarity for the next 3 years,' and if I ask you to prove it, you must have proof. So if you are confident of the subject and you can help people but have no proof, then what you need to do is maybe write a book, or make a few videos , start a YouTube channel, start writing a blog and do what it takes to build credibility for your expertise on the subject. Another way of building credibility is testimonials.

Testimonials

Anybody you have helped in your life, can give you a testimonial. You can ask your friends, family, anybody for it, anybody you have worked with. These testimonials can be in any form, written or video, but try to get video testimonials because they work better. Your testimonial recording should be directly from mic to camera.

Nowadays with the technology of camera and mic, it is inexpensive to get these kind of testimonials. The sound clarity you usually get when you use a mic is of great quality; therefore when you get the testimonials on phone, you can connect a mic to it. Don't ask them to directly sell your programme in the testimonials because they would not sound convincing. Ask them to give their name, background, reason why they attended your programme, and what transformation they got out of the programme.

And then if you want, you can ask them questions and then edit the video. Don't ask them to give lectures or content. Let the background be elegant, with a plant or a painting to make it look nice. And never keep your pictures on the sides of the stage.

I'VE BEEN INVITED FOR TWO EVENTS, IN BEED AND AMBEJOGAI. THERE WERE MORE THAN 4,000 PEOPLE IN THESE EVENTS. PEOPLE WERE STANDING OUTSIDE THE AUDITORIUM JUST TO LISTEN TO ME. FEELING GREAT. SOME PEOPLE ASKED ABOUT MY PAID EVENTS TOO. THANK YOU ARFEEN AND THE STF GROUP.

ANAND BANSODE, EVEREST CLIMBER

ADAPTING YOURSELF TO CHANGE THROUGH THE ACQUISITION OF NEWER SKILLS AND KNOWLEDGE IS PARAMOUNT TO YOUR FUTURE.

4

Building Your Audience

If you get any content from a book or somebody else, it won't work as it is not your content. Trainers use other people's content and transformation experts build their own stories to create content. Your story will define your tribe.

Do you watch all movies that are released? No! There are some movies you watch because your favourite actor or actress is in it, or maybe because you like that kind of movie. I like Amitabh Bachchan, so I watch his movies for sure. I like Hrithik Roshan, so I watch his movies. Salman Khan I like, I watch his movies as well. Shah Rukh I might watch, or I might not. Aamir Khan for sure, I would watch all of his movies. Anything with KK Menon, Irfan khan and Paresh Rawal would come out and I would watch it definitely just because they have worked in it.

I am the tribe of KK Menon, Irfan Khan, Amitabh Bachchan, Hrithik Roshan, Salman Khan, these are the ones that would drive me to watch a movie. If there is a movie on, I am going to rush there. If a Shah Rukh Khan movies comes up I am not going to rush for the movie unless I am really interested in the subject.

Every story has a tribe. If you were to have me market a movie on Facebook, what movie would you choose for me? Obvious, right? Because my tribe is defined!

What trainers and speakers do generally is they come out with a very broad subject; they market it to everyone and hope somebody buys. This is something silly; instead define your tribe based on the story. If you have got a story that is yours and it is powerful, you can take out the content of your story and make it into a transformational programme and people who want to hear your story would come.

Will I go to a programme on how to look young at 70?
No, I won't be interested.

Would I go to a programme on how to talk a woman in 3 minutes?
Maybe.

Will I go to aprogramme on how to lose 20 kilograms?
No!

So, your story has to be defined by a specific tribe. If you don't have a story, build a story. If you interview 50 people on a particular subject, you get enough experience about that subject. I will now have enough content to have the confidence to teach that subject to anybody.

If I start writing a book about it and I start building more content, of course I will have some element of the story or I would not pick that subject. If I was in your place and was to choose a subject, I would definitely go out of my way and interview people; it is the most powerful way for you to get leverage. When you write a book, you ask for testimonials from famous or credible people; but you could do the same thing with the people around you: you could go and interview them. Imagine you are sitting in a car, you get the camera rolling and talk to someone while they are driving or in the backseat of the car and interview them; talk on the streets and interview people. And this is going to give you great content to talk about.

What do you want to do: (tribe)

After you plan your 1-month, 6-month or a 1-year programme, you need to do certain things for your digital product. The formula is:

Content = Your Story + what the market wants.

Your story ingredients: choosing your ultimate story.

What would you love to teach?

Let's leave your experiences aside, and if you had the opportunity to teach anything on earth, it need not be motivational or inspirational. We had one couple that came to our Speak To a Fortune programme and they wanted to teach how to have a natural birth at home instead of going to the hospital. You could teach people how to dance and transform yourself, you could teach people how to paint and create transformations for yourself. It could be anything.

Do you know there is a therapy in which they give you very difficult designs and drawings with very minute details to colour. At times, they also have numbers that you have to fill in. And it is proven that colouring these books gives you tremendous focus and clarity on life in general. You get these colouring books in all the book stores now; they are very popular.

While you are colouring, what are you thinking about? Nothing! You are so focused on colouring the minute details that you can't think of anything else. It takes you away from your entire world and keeps you engrossed in the moment. If you spend an hour a day, doing these colours, you will have a mega transformation of in your life because it removes you from the stress of life and living. Remember, you are not supposed to heal people or counsel them; you are supposed to help them reach the next level.

Depressed people would never come to you for help because they have lost the motivation to do so. We are here to help people. If you ask me what topic I would like to teach, I would like to take a seminar where somebody can help me get 20,000 people in a room. That's a problem I have now, but I am not going to fall on the ground right now.

Some people would like to work with people who are abused; that would be something like counselling and not what you do on a grand scale because you can't advertise that, as it won't work. The language you use has to be exciting. If I ask you to draw a picture of something, I guarantee you would draw a picture of your life in some way or the other.

The more experiences you have, the quicker your seminar will sell. And never forget, when you are teaching people, it's not only about content, it's about experience, it's about excitement, it's about fun. The more games, the more experiences you have, the more quickly your seminar will sell.

The more experiences you give, the quicker your coaching will work. In fact, if you could do a programme where you have nothing but activity after activity, with a break in between with learning, you can have a great seminar. It's not about giving a Wikipedia of content; that is what people do generally, they give so much content that it becomes boring.

I want you all to remember that everything you are going to create is going to be based on your stories and experiences and that's when you will become a powerful transformational expert. You are not a trainer and you are not doing motivational speaking. You are doing transformation and people pay very well for transformation.

Let me ask you a question: *what would you do for free if you could work for free.* Now that doesn't mean what topic you would teach. What we are trying to work out here is finding your inner voice to discover what we can create from it.

For example, I have a Speak To a Fortune participant in Delhi who loves photography, he loves to ride motorbikes, and he wants to make people happy. So what he did is...

he went on a 5,000 miles journey around India on his bike, taking pictures of people smiling and asking them why are they smiling. What a journey! If he wanted to, he could write a really awesome book, he could do an excellent programme; he could actually become an expert on happiness. That idea came across during my Speak To a Fortune seminar he was attending, and it came out of his passion for photography, his passion for motorbikes and his passion to make people happy.

Similarly, you can take your passion and go around the country like this. You have to just think about your topic. It can be anything that you are passionate about.

Another question to be asked is: On what do your friends, family and other people seek advice?

People who know you and are close to you, what do they come to you for? These are the people that know you very well and know what you can deal with. My niece calls me up whenever she has a problem. Problems like: 'My mom won't listen to me,' or, 'My friend is going through this problem.' If you share your personal experiences in your seminar, people will always give you a great response. If you go on stage and share these, there would be 0% denial or doubt from the audience. When the stories and the experiences are powerful, you can use both and create an outcome for somebody.

You can inspire people with your story. Everybody has a story and these stories are really powerful if you understand them.

Six to seven years ago, I was in London watching on TV the news of massive earthquakes in Pakistan, and felt terrible. But just sitting in front of a TV and feeling terrible meant I was not doing anything about it. Then I went to my dad and told him I was going to Pakistan. He asked me why I was going to Pakistan, and rather advised me to skip the idea as there was much trouble between India and

Pakistan at that time. I told him I wanted to go because of the earthquakes there and I wanted to help people and I felt I could do something useful there.

At first, he was reluctant to let me go, but then he gave me permission to travel out. So, I got my visa and I arrived on day 3 of the earthquake in Islamabad, a very beautiful city indeed. And I thought of ways to help, I thought of finding an NGO. So I found a cybercafé, searched for NGOs and found four or five of them. Each one said no space. I searched some more and I found one and they said I had to get vaccinated. I declined because I don't go in for vaccinations but somehow I convinced them to take me in.

I reached the place in the Northwest Frontier in an area called Balakot and on arrival, I was told that thousands of people had been killed. And as I looked around, I couldn't see any destruction anywhere. All I could see were the most amazing and beautiful mountainous areas. The location was just breathtaking. On speaking with the people, I learnt that among all these hills and mountains, there were villages that had been sliced off and people in the valleys had been crushed to death.

So, then we went to this location and I found a piece of land and set up our camp. And the NGO decided we were going to set up 200 tents with beds and a hospital to treat the injured while I wondered where the injured were? Then we set out for the main town of Balakot and it was like a Bollywood movie.

Imagine driving up to a city, stepping out of your, come to an edge and in front of you is a very big town and there is nothing left of it but just flattened buildings. The whole town is demolished! It is such a shock sight for me that I fall on my knees and start crying my eyes out.

I had never seen destruction apart from in the movies; it was scary. My brain could not compute the magnitude of the destruction. Then we went down and I could hear people screaming, people stuck under the debris, people dying; and I wondered what to do.

Over the next 30 days, I took out hundreds of dead school children, met people with legs full of pus. I had to get a knife and cut the wounds open and stitch up people, something I had never done before in my life. We climbed hills, met people who lived in families; they ate what they produced. There was no ambition there, they did what they had to, to sustain themselves. Then there were families that had completely wiped out. One day, I saw this forlorn woman sitting somewhere, and went up to her.

'What happened?'

'Do you see those 4 doomed places?' She pointed at a distance. 'Those aremy husband and my three children. I had to drag them out of the house and bury them myself.'

I stared at her speechless as she said, 'You know what… God is great, everything happens for a reason, no one could have done anything about this and I have to move on.'

I thought to myself: 'How can someone possibly do that?' I looked around and only saw destruction.

I didn't shower for 20 days because it was freezing. I remember going to this small town and seeing this hair dresser there who advertised 'Hot shower at 20 rupees. 'As I went into that shower I realised how grateful I was to be having this shower. People were walking 50kms up and down in the hills for a bag of daal, a bag of rice and biscuits.

And then I saw camps from Cuba, the United States, Australia, India and all other countries in this area. And all out there helping and supporting people. The experience was a game changer for me, because in my head, it brought home the reality of the life I lead.

While I was at Balakot, my paternal aunt whom I was very close to passed away, but I had already seen so much death around me recently that I did not cry.

Balakot changed my life forever. That was the time when I changed my focus. It took me away from 'me' to 'what can I do'. This, despite everyone telling me to not go to Pakistan, despite people telling me if I went there and I'd fall sick.

Somethings were indeed sickening: amidst all the destruction, guys were walking around with machine guns; biscuits meant for relief were being sold in the shops for a premium, people were stealing money, even jewellery from the dead bodies. I witnessed the corrupt face of mankind truly up-close.

By now I had become a little known there because of my work. I started coaching people and helping doctors especially because they were traumatised by what they saw. One day, a general of that area called me up. And they took me in a helicopter for an aerial survey of the devastation before taking me to a hospital.

They had found a man alive after 27 days; somehow he had survived and was in a very bad condition. His body was stiff like a rock and they told me, I had to make him speak. I said I couldn't do that as I didn't know how to do it. Then in my mind I said ,'Why shouldn't I have a go?'

He was a very old man just sitting there and I would try hard to talk to him. Every day I would visit him and hope to get him to say a word. Nothing happened!

Days before I was leaving, my brother had also come by. He spent some 20 days there and fortunately by the time I left, the old man had begun to utter a few words. Again I completely broke down because I realised the old man was desperate to just hear a few comforting words. And I wondered when was the last time I went to my parents and told them I cared about them. They would be desperate to hear that. When was the last time I told my sister and brother and friends and other people that I know and are close to me that I care about them?

I remember when we were taking out a little girl, a kid on the school desk who must have been studying and her head was flat on the desk and she was dead with a pen in her hand. That's how swiftly it had happened. So, this experience of mine changed my world. It changed me like you can't imagine. It changed me beyond my imagination.

If I took that experience now and shared that to produce a specific outcome, people would be impacted. That experience was a journey, I could actually help people on how to handle difficult times, I could do a seminar on gratitude, and I could do a million things based on that one story.

Have I now earned the right?

I have!

I have a 7-hour video footage, where in, I have gone to people and I have asked them about their experiences and what was going on and the one thing I discovered at that moment is despite the chaos and the calamity, people were just very hopeful about life. At times like these, you embrace your responsibilities and pain and say 'God knows best.' What a quick and simple way for people to move on. So your story and your experiences can help people.

Why do people come to me? They don't come to me for advice. They come to me because they know this person is going to reframe something in a different way, I am going to spin it or change it and come up with a new solution. I don't give advice because I am not good at doing that. If you come to me with a problem, I will come out with a new version of looking at it. I change people's perspective and that's what I do best.

The question to ask is when do your friends, family and other people seek your advice? And if they don't come to you, there is a problem. No matter your age, people always come to you with their problems. The more you are able to express your stories, the more powerful speaker you are going to be.

Everything I share with you is in the past and I am not ashamed of that. I talk about the fact that I lost money, I was broke and more, but I am not this anymore. So you should not have a problem talking about your past. Some people say they don't want to say they are divorced because other would think badly of them or they don't want to mention about difficult times or people would think they are weak.

Have you seen *The Pursuit of Happiness*?

Why we do like that story or what is so great about that movie – because of its ups and downs? Everybody likes stories which evoke the feeling of rising from the ashes into the sky like a Phoenix.

When you are on stage and you are sharing your story about how difficult it life once was. I remember when I had dengue fever and I was in the hospital, it was one of the worst experiences I had ever had in my life. I started thinking maybe I would not come through this and I started thinking of what was good in my life. I even wrote a letter and put it under my pillow thinking even if I popped off, my family would get that letter. But what a game changer it turned out for me; when I came out of the hospital, I got another chance.

If you look at Jim Rohn, his entire programme is a story – my daddy used to do this and my mom used to do this and my friends used to do this. You can get emotional about your topic and the audience actually thinks that you actually mean what you say; you become authentic. You have to be yourself on stage, that's why actors like Amitabh Bachchan are successful. Whenever he has done an angry role, he has done it really well. If you look at his trends, he has delivered blockbusters when he has played the angry young man.

Someone like Irfan Khan is not very different from himself when he acts, and delivers such convincing performances.

If I want to cast Amitabh Bachchan in a movie and if I want it to be a super hit, I have to make a film about an angry young man. Don't be scared to be vulnerable; if you are scared to be vulnerable then it is going to be difficult for you to share that connection. You have to get used to telling your stories again and again but every time you tell it, you have to feel them because they are real.

Which book do you wish to write?

The set of books that I like are the ones that I really resonate with. My favourite book is the *Law of Success* by Napoleon Hill. Had he not written it, I would have written it, if you know what I mean; it is my kind of book. I like *The Secret* and *The Master Key System*. I would like to write such books. I also like this book, *The Millionaire Next Door*. Whenever you are thinking of books, think of books that you would had written and it will give you a lot more ideas on what kind of a subject you should do.

When I say what I want to learn, I would want to understand more about how people express emotions. I am learning something called micro expressions right now. If you have heard of Paul Ekman, he is an expert in micro expressions.

So if I talk to you and I see a sudden shift in your cheek or if I see a blushing happening, it's not body language reading, it's a very minute way to represent one of the six emotions: anger, disgust, fear, sadness, surprise and happiness. It's a really good art but it will probably take me three years to learn it or maybe even five years, but that is something I want to go towards. You should think of stuff that is going to be your growth and what you are going to learn eventually. Ideas can be very different; not a subject of a broad sweep but something very niche. I went to a programme by a person called Gottman, he is a very good psychologist and he teaches about how you can handle post-traumatic growth: there is post-traumatic stress disorder, where people go through post-traumatic growth.

People go through massive trauma; they actually go through massive growth sometimes. And there is another programme on how you can handle relationship challenges, for example, conflict resolution.

So I went on a programme on how I can help people resolve conflict. I wanted to learn that because I know, conflict comes up very frequently in many relationships. So, I am trying to think ahead on what information I would want to learn. You can devise your future based on the learnings you want to do. Don't do what everyone is doing. There is so much knowledge out there, you cannot even imagine; things that are unique and brilliant that people don't even know about. Do your research and spend time on doing that.

Many of you will not get a perfect topic or subject, it will evolve. Think about a specific area, if you could spend three months or six months or a year working with somebody, what you could from take them. What transformation would you want to create in yourself? Come in as a person and walk out as somebody else. What would be that transformation and the answer has to come basically from your content, which you have been thinking of so far.

Have you seen the movie *Yaarana* (1995)? There is a very funny scene in it, where Amitabh Bachchan comes to the big city and Amjad Khan goes into the elevator; the elevator goes up and comes down and an old person walks out of the elevator. Amitabh goes crazy thinking that an elevator is a machine that makes a person grow old. Getting the right subject can sometimes take time. If you are confused it is ok, because confusion means you are thinking. When you go to buy a painting, you might get confused on which painting to buy as you like too many of them, but you can buy one painting and change it later. Similarly, if you don't get your perfect subject right now, at least you can go through the process and get to a point.

The method I am telling you may take a bit of time but in the long run, you will have a long-term business. People must know you by one specific transformation. I always give examples of actors: Amitabh Bachchan – Angry Young Man; Salman Khan – The Dude; Shah Rukh Khan – King of Romance; Aamir Khan – Mr. Perfect. All these superstars are known for a single transformation. Paresh Rawal – comedy, villain everything, but he is not a superstar; Irfan Khan – all-rounder; KK Menon, Nawazuddin Siddiqui have been doing a variety of roles, but not been associated with a particular niche. When you have too many subjects, you have too much to give and when you have too much to give, narrowing down to something more niche is a problem. Therefore, when you are beginning, create an identity; once you gain visibility you may add more topics.

I am not telling you not to do any other subject. Tony Robbins started with phobias. He went on radio and challenged people to bring him any phobia and he would fix that and he would do it in seconds. After this, what made Tony Robbins famous was the 'Fire Walk'. No one had done it before and everybody was agog that this man could make anybody walk on fire and he removed phobia. He is a magician, he can make magic happen and over the years you build up and build up and build up. Initially he was just 'Mr. Phobia'; he went around the country telling people he could fix anything. He would get a snake or a spider and give someone to hold it.

Once you get famous, you can do seminars on any topic and it doesn't matter. Whatever you want to do, but at least get there first. What kind of cars does Ferrari make? High performance, sports cars. You can get a sports car for $10,000 also but there will be only a few Ferraris, Lamborghinis, McLarens or Bugattis. Which one are you? What are you known for? Ferrari's identity is the horse.

So what is your identity, be narrow, pick one subject. I know one person who has a complete seminar on how to resolve an argument. Books, DVD, everything you can imagine and only part of the relationship – how to overcome an argument. You should be marketing the simplest things in the world. You need to come out with things like 'Oh my God, this guy has crashed, and we need to raise him.' What I am saying is create an identity around a specific issue.

Health, fitness, money, public-speaking, financial freedom, wellness, money, sales, happiness, spirituality, parenting, food, mindfulness, stress management, children, parenting, beauty, weight loss, anti-aging, baking, relationships – these are the important subjects in which you can achieve massive success every single time. Even if you take one aspect of it, you can become wealthy in that. And I am not telling you to stick to one subject; I am saying build up your identity and do whatever you want to do. People say you should dress up in a certain way, I can wear a pair of shorts and do my training, and no one is going to complain about it to me. Once you build up an identity, no one cares.

If I ask somebody in the morning why they go to work, the answer will be – because they have to pay bills and that's not very exciting. What is your greater purpose? What message are you here to serve the world? Most people don't think like that. The root cause is that people are being told: 'When you grow up, get a job, earn money, buy a house, get married, have children, get them married,' and so on. It's about time people are told, 'When you grow up, you need to make a difference in the world, you need to make an impact in your family, you need to be extraordinary.'

My dad told me to take charge of my life and to not give up and always work for yourself. But most people around are never told this, they are told to get a job.‘ Without education you will do nothing in life.’ Nobody is ever told to focus on themselves. Has anyone ever told their kids to grow up and become a philosopher or grow up and become an artist or a musician; people don’t do that.

Most of them will ask you to study, get a good education, do a graduation, be secure in life. I am saying, doing something you want to will be adventurous, and ask urge you to create variety in life, to create meaning in life, to identify your purpose in life.

The reason why Google is doing so well is if you go to Google office, and if you see the engagement there, it is insane. These people really know how to keep their employees engaged. They have all the facilities available in the world, they have food available everywhere and it is free in most cases, organic vegetables, organic fruits, they have laundry and everything available for you. You can pick your colours and design your office in most cases. Such is the engagement that nobody wants to leave them. What I am saying is look at what you are planning to teach. What is in demand; tell your story and prove that you can help with it.

Some people realise that one day when they were down and they started dancing, dancing took them out of a state of being down and out to a state of freedom. So they can teach people how to dance to become free. Don’t complicate life; choose simpler subjects.

When you come on stage and show vulnerability, then you show the solution, people will connect with you. And when they connect with you, they will believe you and they will take charge of their life with everything you say, because they can relate to you. If Usain Bolt, the runner, said: ‘When I first started, I could not really run but I put together this amazing system that can make any person become a runner and you know my background is that I come from a very poor family, I didn't know if I could do this, and I had a trainer, he pushed me, drove me and today I am the fastest man on earth. I run more than 10 mtrs in under a second,' and if he gave advice to an upcoming runner, would they listen to him or would they doubt him? If he came up with a programme that would cost somewhere around $10,000 and is only limited to 10 people and if they do not have money, what would they do?

They would beg, borrow and steal and do anything to get that $10,000 because the credibility of Usain Bolt and his programme is that high. And what if I tell you I have a programme and I will teach you the psychology of running because I have interviewed the top 10 runners of the world and they have told me what their blueprint is as they run and they have told me what they think and do as they run, you would pay me anything I ask for. Create something out of your story.

There is a programme called 'Tough Mudder'; it is an insane challenge: around 5000 people they jump into ice-cold water, they go into electrical wires, they climb up unimaginable places. Some people break their legs along the way, last year an Indian died of heart attack over there. 5000 people go insane each year on that challenge just to complete it, not to win it and people would pay for that.

The Iron Man's Challenge, the Devil Circuit…there are all these crazy ideas and more, and people are ready to take them up. You need to pick a simple topic and conduct a seminar on it, and people will pay for it. But if you do too many seminars and too many subjects, you will become a master of none and a junkie. I have been there and done that. I had a list of about 20 different programmes on my menu for people to choose from. And I was a trainer but I didn't want to do that.

I FEEL SO GRATEFUL TO YOU FOR THIS ACCOMPLISHMENT. THE BEST THING THAT I HAVE LEARNT FROM YOU IS TO ALWAYS KEEP MY FOCUS OUTWARD AND ARFEEN, DUE TO THIS, IN MY FIRST WORKSHOP ITSELF, I HAD TWO MAJOR BREATHROUGHS: I FELT HAPPIER THAN THEM, FOR THEM. IN THAT MOMENT, I REALISED THIS IS MY PURPOSE AND I CAN'T THANK YOU ENOUGH FOR MAKING ME MEET...MYSELF.

VARSHA NALIN SHAH, HAPPINESS ENGINEER

THE JOURNEY OF A THOUSAND MILES BEGINS WITH A STEP, FOLLOWED BY ANOTHER. SIMILARLY, YOU HAVE TO BUILD YOUR LIFE, BIT BY BIT, ONE DAY AFTER ANOTHER.

5

The Transformational Content

How to put together your content? Many people think that giving information is what people pay for. People don't pay for information, they can get it on Google for free. Many speakers/trainers only keep giving information but these kind of things don't make money. Transformational experts don't do that. Transformational experts will provide solutions.

For example, I know one person who wants to take a topic like relationships and narrow it down married couples: 'How to Build Happy Marriages'. This again being a vast topic, to further narrow it down, he chose 'How to Manage Anger Between Couples.'

This is an awesome subject and will do really well. He is going to help couples resolve anger issues in their relationship. He was married for almost two years; it was a love marriage, yet he could not understand his partner and there was much discord. There came a time where he actually wanted to get divorced and move on in life.

Now with time, he has the most amazing relationship; his partner is his best friend and more than a wife, and he can really sense what she means to him. He knows the structure that he has lived through, so he wants to have a workshop where he wants to take all couples who have issues in their relationship for a five-to-six-day seminar. And he wants to do some activities with them so they all come closer and resolve their issues, develop understanding and work on their lives.

It is not about changing the partner; it is about working on the emotional quotient. He plans to do this seminar together with his wife so they can inspire people. He is very passionate about his topic.

I think it's a very popular subject and many people do not know how to resolve anger issues in their marriage. It is a big problem for people. Some people are very reactionary, some will attack, some people will co-ordinate, some will scratch and some will just go silent in anger. And all this affects the family as well. Parents' relationship have an impact on their children as well. I know a couple, and every time the couple had an argument, the wife would bite him. That's scary.

At this moment, if you don't have a subject in your mind, make one up and it is probably the right subject. But you should be passionate about your topic. No acting, no presentation; but there should be a feel in your eyes and your voice when you say it. There should be an engagement with the audience where everybody just listens to you; all this should be a part of you. The only reason some of you will not get your subject is that you are trying to make it perfect. There can be no other reason.

As I have said earlier, choosing a subject is like buying a painting. You can always change the painting whenever you want. After a few months, you may realise that this isn't the thing that you want. You are allowed to change your painting all the time. Don't panic if you don't come out with a subject. Make it up and it's probably the subject that you want to do because you cannot make up something that you don't want to do.

Now let's create a very basic framework of a course. Whenever you decide to write a new programme, you need to follow a tool. Suppose you want to make a new product, a digital product, a DVD or a seminar, any programme, you can use the following to create a very basic framework of your programme:

Course Title

When it comes to making a course title, the ingredients to making a good title are that it should be catchy. For example, 'Speak To A Fortune'; It should sound good and interesting. People may call it 'Train The Trainer' but that's boring. My programme was named this earlier but everyone is doing 'Train The Trainer' and my programme is instantly compared to it.

Let's define a catchy name for 'How to Build Happy Marriages'. If you are in a relationship and you are angry and you are attacking or you are shouting or screaming all the time, then he is the man to look out for. If he walks into your house, there will be bliss and harmony. What can we call this man's programme?

How about 'Rekindle Your Relationship'? 'Rekindle' is a nice word that makes you feel very warm. Don't choose titles that are negative or unclear. Don't keep any sad titles either. They just put off people.

Okay so let's do an exercise; imagine you are on Facebook and an ad appears on the right-hand side and you see the picture of a young man and he is saying 'After my programme…', and the list of all the anger breakthroughs – 'you will not bite someone again, you will not scream or shout…' etc. and as you read the content of that seminar, it gets you really excited and at the count of three you go back up to the headline and imagine the name of this seminar.

For example, 'Angry Birds in Love', I can imagine two angry birds looking at each other and a shadow of a heart between them or something like that. If the title is unclear, we need a tagline to this title so that it will give more clarity on what the programme is about. It can be something like 'Come and Rediscover Your Love', or 'Seven Steps to Change Anger into Passion', or 'A Unique Way to Make Anger Disappear'.

Your tagline should not be too long or dramatic; it should give a clear idea of what the seminar is about. In a line, it should describe what the programme is about.

This programme helps resolve anger, so it should specify this in the tagline itself and I want the audience to know that there is a formula and there is something very unique. I want you to know that this programme will help you get rid of your anger and there is a system and I want you think, 'Oh my god, there is a system to it' and I want you to know about the unique system or process of making anger your friend, a unique process of combating anger and transforming it into something constructive. When somebody reads the subject title and tagline, they should be eager to know what it is all about. Everybody wants a magic trick, everyone just wants a formula. If you are able to put a title with a little tagline that can give you some emphasis about the power in your formula, it makes things easier.

Give your audience a taste of something extraordinary; it's like telling your audience, 'Listen, I have something that is unique.' Even the word 'magic' may sound corny; people love it but the seminar better be magical, and it better produce a result, otherwise people will think you are bullshitting them. Avoid words like 'magic'. 'Instant' is fine as are words like 'formula', 'process', 'unique' because when I say 'formula,' you will automatically assume it to be a magic quotient.

Think of a tagline and give it a meaning and if title of your programme is crystal clear, you don't need to have a tagline. If your title means a million things, you need to clarify your subject with the help of a tagline. Like 'Speak To A Fortune' is not crystal clear' that is why I have a tagline that says 'Make A Fortune Teaching What You Love.' That clarifies the subject: that this is something about teaching/coaching and making money.

QUICK RESULTS. 620 REGISTERED ON FACEBOOK. 60 PEOPLE WERE PRESENT TODAY. I SOLD A TWO-DAY SEMINAR FOR RS. 12,500. 13 REGISTERED. 12 PAID. ONE TO PAY TOMORROW. MENTIONED ABOUT 1-YEAR COACHING PROGRAMME. I MENTIONED I CHARGE 5 LACS FOR IT AND THAT IT IS ONLY FOR THE SELECT FEW THAT I CHOOSE. ONE INTERESTED IN THE 1-YEAR PROGRAMME AND REQUESTING ME TO TAKE HER AS MY MENTEE. MY EXPERIENCE IS AM FEELING GREAT. STRONGER SELF-BELIEF AND BELIEF IN A SYSTEM. ARFEEN, I AM LOOKING FORWARD TO MEETING YOU. LOTS TO DO AND LEARN.

REETA SHAH, SUPERWOMAN

STRENGTH LIES IN
A STEADY MIND.

6

Creating Your First Programme and Digital Content

How to Structure Your Programme

Think of a title for your programme. What could you call your programme? I will give you some examples of mine. I have got a 'Secret Millionaire Blueprint', nice name and it is pretty clear what it is, it's a blueprint on how to become a millionaire and it's a secret. The word 'secret' makes you think about what it is. I have got 'Speak To A Fortune' which is not so clear but it still sounds quite good. I have got a 'Mental Warrior' which is pretty clear again, 'Call Of Destiny' is not so clear but I think it's a really nice name. I am assuming it means going towards my destiny. Then I have 'Elite Retreat' which is a luxurious programme to places so unique that you will never go there.

Once I went to a programme in South Africa and I had dinner at Nelson Mandela's house. He wasn't there but with me on the table were 15 other people, with this person playing the violin in the background; and sitting at the other end of the table was the world's fastest cheetah. Of course, he was one of the captured cheetahs but he was sitting at the table while we were having dinner.

And it was amazing, I was having dinner at Nelson Mandela's house, so that is a kind of place in 'Elite Retreat' that we take you to. You will fly to a location, get picked up in a helicopter, be taken to an island, and you will have dinner in a monastery that is in middle of an island that you will never ever go to. You will meet some people that otherwise you would never meet. We would take you to the African jungles or some unique places that you would never visit. And these are unique experiences. The name is 'Elite Retreat' and it is very clear.

I have one another programme called 'Transformation Of The Mindset' which, as the title suggests, is about transforming your mindset. It is crystal clear. You should come up with names that are very clear and exciting. Don't forget it's like a painting and you can change it anytime you want.

Don't call yourself a trainer or don't call yourself a coach, call yourself something unique like 'Happiness Engineer'. One of my participants goes with that name and she's become so successful, she was even a part of TEDx!

30 Questions

I am going to give you the magic formula now and this is what I have been teaching for a long time; it is so simple that most of you will never do it. For you to make content, this is the template you need to follow and this is all you need to do for your entire life in your profession.

The formula is called the 30-points formula. I am going to tell you the difference between someone who is a trainer and someone who is a transformational expert. The content you will put together will be these 30-questions.

A trainer will give you knowledge and information and a transformational expert will give you solutions. Solutions to what?

Let's take an example, of 'How to Build Happy Marriages', his subject is resolving challenges faced in relationships due to anger and his audience is couples.

Now imagine you are in a marriage and both the people are consistently fighting but they love each other, or they love each other but can't stand each other. Because they come home and they fight and they go away and they think if it could work, it would be so nice and they go back and they fight again. They care but the thought of going home could mean another fight for them. Imagine someone you know or yourself in that situation. You can know more about how to ask those 30 questions in my Speak To a Fortune programme; just go here: speaktofortune/letter.

How to Create Products

Talking about products, you could make an anger management kit or a DVD programme or maybe anger flash cards or you could pick one of these topics and talk about it when you go somewhere as a guest speaker.

And you don't need any qualifications to do this. I am not qualified; I do have some certificates and a degree, but I don't think that is what I needed to do this. This involves Psychology but you are not dealing with psychopaths or mentally ill people, you are dealing with people who are angry in their relationships and for this, your experience and your stories are enough. If you present these in a powerful way and people follow your system, it will work.

My theory when I get angry is, I just sit down and if it is possible to sit on the floor then it is even better because you look completely stupid when you sit on the floor angry and when I sit down, my heart rate slows down. Then I have my wife sitting in front of me going nuts and I see this big red nose coming on her face and I am looking at her and all I am looking at is the big red nose and she is obviously wondering what the hell am I looking at because this is quite annoying.

This is kind a diversion. Earlier, I used to have a red nose in my pocket and I would put it on and it did work for a while and then she got irritated. That is my anger management. I can get a balloon and pop it in front of her, that might shock her a bit or in the middle of the fight I can tell her, 'You know what, someone called me today and said you are a very nice person,' and she will start asking who called and she would get diverted. There are so many diversionary tactics that I can use.

The point I am trying to put forward is this system is not what you will be taught by a counsellor or a psychologist and not that they are always right. But I know that if someone did this, it would work and if you can resolve anger. If you are confused about your topic, and want to have a breakthrough, I would suggest you come to my Speak To a Fortune 3-month programme; just go here to get the special price: speaktofortune/letter.

If I want to do a programme on health today, then I can do it easily.

1. Be aware of what you are eating; take a picture of every meal that you eat for the next 10 days.
2. Increase your water intake.
3. Have an Hour of Power – sit down for an hour and do absolutely nothing. If someone calls you and asks what you are doing, say 'nothing'.
4. Try to burn at least 500 calories a day through brisk walking or running.
5. Have a very good Vitamin and minerals intake.

And there's so much more…

If I give this information, I know people's health will improve. It works because I know most people don't burn 500 calories, most people don't have proper intake of Vitamins and minerals, most people don't drink enough water a day, most people don't spend an Hour of Power and most people don't track their food.

If I manage to get you on a system where you have to send me photographs every day of the meals you eat, send me pictures of calorie burn every day and photographs of the water you drink and your word that you are doing your 'Hour of Power,' your life is going to change. People will pay me for this and would say that my health system is most incredible in the world. It doesn't have to be rocket science. It can be very simple.

Simplicity is where the key is. The simpler it is, the more people will do it, the more complicated it is, lesser people will do it.

Everyone is working and everybody has challenges, so don't give a reason why can't you do it; you have to give a reason why can you do it. If you can't do seminars, it is fine, you can do one-to-one or group coaching, you can do strategy sessions or you can do videos, audios…anything you find easier to do.

Even if you decide you are going to do your first seminar a year from now, you can spend the whole year building up this story and preparing for what you are going to present; there is no rush but don't ever come to a point saying, 'I have only started, when I have done my first programme.' That's not when you start, you start now!

Your first video, your first audio, your first podcast or whatever you are going to do, you have to start now. Lot of people judge their success when they do their first seminar but I would say, 'Judge your success by the story you build.'

'Is my story built? Have I built enough evidence to know that I am the best?' and then you know that you can do it!

When people start referring to you as the person who does XYZ, then you know you have achieved it. While that could take a bit of time, if you go fast and efficiently, you could do it in a month.

In one, month you can make 20 videos, you could write a book – a 70 to 80-page book. Studies have shown that the books that are under 90 or 70 pages are read by 70% of the people. So, small books work really very well. You can do 30 small books with the questions that you have. If you can't write books, you can speak out on an audio and transcribe it and that's what I did with my first book. I spoke it and then I got it transcribed. Your journey should begin now and you should say this to yourself every day, 'What task have I done today to build my story?' and over a period of time, it will happen.

You can now form your 30 questions and then you can have a structure for your programme and you can start delivering easily. If you don't have a topic, make it up. Whether you think it is a right topic or not is a different story and it requires only your own approval if you think somebody will be benefited by it. As I have said earlier, you can always change it later.

Decide a topic and ask yourself 'What is the problem that you will solve?' 'What will be the outcome?' 'Who are the people who shall want to come to your programme?' 'What do you want to be known as?' and 'What is the one thing you can solve every single time?' After answering these questions and deciding your topic, come up with your 30 questions!

The Programme Format

You can take your seminars in any language you want. The Hindi market, Gujarati market, Marathi market or Punjabi market, they are all awesome. Do not think that English is the only market.

Maybe in a year or two, I will do a programme in Hindi. That's my goal and if I can do it, you have absolutely no excuse at all. And now I will tell you how your 30 questions will help you. This is a template that will give you synopsis of your entire programme.

If you are using Facebook, you can utilise this content; if a video, you can use the programme format. This can be used for practically everything you do in order to describe your programme.

In my STF programme, suppose I have a programme in January, May and September. So I have a programme every 3 months. The format of the programme is identical. So when you come back to another 5-days programme, there will be no change in format but the content will always be different because it is public driven.

But the good thing is, when I do a preview in November, December and early January, I can sell my programme that starts in January end. I can continue to do my preview in February, March. A fair number of strategy sessions, one-to-one or free seminars, and I can get people to my May event. I can continue in June, July, August and I can get people to my September event. And I do this every single month.

I can do a preview somewhere and market the same programme that I have all round the year, which means I am not limited. What people generally do is they put in place a six-month programme, they market it in January and they can never sell a programme until June.

And if I for example have 5 people joining in January, I can have another 25 in May and another 10 in September maybe and by the end of the year maybe 80 people in total. So I can market this programme all year long and never worry about having enough people for my programme.

If I want, I can create a funnel to market a book first or a digital product and market my programme there eventually. But the key is to have an evergreen programme.

Your three-month programme has to be based on tools and processes through which you will get results. If you would like to do a two-day workshop, let me give you a formula for that: you can make a two-day workshop into a three-month programme. You do two days of workshop and three months of assignments.

The difference is that the value of the programme is three times better as you are still doing that two-day programme and having three months of assignments and maybe in between, you can have a video call or maybe a get-together in a video shop, it becomes a much more valuable programme that would cost you nothing, you can have your processes and assignments pre-written, you can either email them, you can send it to them or whatever you want to do and this is how your two-day programme becomes a three-month programme.

Even if you charge 10-15,000 for a two-day programme, you can easily charge a 40-50,000 for a three-month programme and I guarantee you, people will pay. And you just don't bullshit them because the programme is bigger, you give them value. Remember one thing, when you charge higher for your programmes, you can put more money into your programmes and make them better.

If you do two-day programmes, you can do that five times a year this way. Don't get scared by the three-month word, it can be a two-day programme + three-months-of-assignment programme. Buddy meets are for people to engage with each other. People love that kind of stuff. Group therapy is much better than any one-to-one coaching. Group work is the best in the world because you can learn from each other.

At the beginning you need to stick with one thing only or else you are going to get confused. All I am saying to you is that when I say a three-month programme, do the programmes for actually two days but give people follow up and support for three months. If you want to do a six-months programme, you can do a two-day programme twice with support and tools and books and DVDs and whatever else you want to give.

One thing that you can also do is that you can do a six-month programme which will have two-day programmes thrice during these six months. Let's say there are three different programmes and at the end of the seminar, no one buys the programme. You can sell them first two days of the programme and ask them not to buy the six months; they can just come for the two days and pay 15,000 and experience it. When they come for two days and experience it, they may buy the whole six-month programme. You can take two days out of your six months and sell it individually.

You don't have to keep making new programmes. People need to see value, otherwise they don't want to come.

The outcome of the Millionaire Blueprint Programme is to realise that the money you make will not come from the effort you put on the outside, it works on the effort you make on the inside. It's got nothing to do with hard work but from where you process the information. I also want my audience to know how they are processing information at the current moment and I want to give them a system that they can utilise to reprogramme their brain, That's the outcome and hopefully, they will come to my 'Call of Destiny' programme and that's another outcome. So that's the process I put my audience through when they come to my programme.

Step 1 is always awareness, so:

What is the way you think right now?

What is your life like?

What do you believe about money?

What do you believe about love?

What is your truth?

Step 2 is consequences of your belief.

Step 3 is my formula then

Step 4, Step 5 and then the result…

You want your audience to walk away with outcomes, and when you come to my programme you will.

You don't have to be a speaker to do this business; you just need to get a process. You don't share personal stuff until and unless it's resolved. You don't share something that is currently happening in your life. You can get a little emotional, people will connect with you but you don't have to cry your lungs out, because people are coming for personal growth. Getting emotional is not the key, but being powerful is.

WORKING WITH ARFEEN GIVES YOU THE COURAGE TO DREAM BIG. CAN'T WAIT FOR THE COMING MONTHS TO UNFOLD AND WATCH THE DREAMS TURNING INTO REALITY.

ROHINI MUNDRA, MINDSHIFT COACH

VISUALISE YOUR GOAL AS A TARGET. THEN FOCUS ON IT AND HIT THE TARGET.

7

Strategies to Impact Your Audience

Why do you need to do previews?

Preview is an actual preview to your high-end programme. In the preview, you start with an Introduction to establish that you have the right to teach, because the audience wants to know whether the offer is credible enough for them to spend time listening to to you, because 40% of your time has to be spent on establishing a rapport and this is where people usually go wrong. So when I say rapport, I will build a little bit of history; the quickest way to build rapport is through your personal story.

How to present your story

For example, if I am going to talk about inner strength, I cannot just come and say, 'Ladies and Gentleman, today we are going to talk about inner strength.' I can say, 'You know, there is something so dear to me and let me tell you why. I was bullied in my school and I thought I was weak. Every day I went to school and hoped not to be bullied and it made me weaker and weaker.

'Then as I grew older, I stopped speaking to people because I was always scared that if I get something wrong, people would bully me. And then I had pimples on my face, so people used to call me Pizza Face or Moon Face. There are always a couple of idiots at school and others like them. And at my school there were these two guys who used to carry tape recorders and walk around like dudes and they were the biggest idiots. Idiots get their glory by pushing people down and that's how they get their power, they are evil people.

'As a young kid, I used to like this girl a lot; I was crazy about her. Everybody in the school knew. Even the girl knew but I had never told her anything and it became like a joke and that became a part of the reason I was bullied as well.

'One day someone came to my class saying that the girl is punched and I lost my mind. At that time, my mind didn't give a damn about the bullies and I went hunting for the person who had punched her. I was not even dating this girl but I just wanted to kill this guy. And I came across this group of three bullies and I punched them and I beat the crap out of all three and that was like solid beating and everyone around me wondered what had happened to me. And guess what, the following day on, I became the most popular guy at school.

'My inner confidence was still low because I thought maybe this is just an incident but when the bullies would see me and run, my strength started building up.

'I became strong and I build inner strength. The same thing happened when I started my business. I was doing so well but my business went from 100 crores to zero overnight and I collapsed for 10 minutes. After 10 minutes, I told myself, 'They took my money, they can take my everything, but they can't take my knowledge.' And I decided that the people who attacked me are the people who will love me. So I made friends with all of those people. As a result, my inner strength grew. This is an example of building rapport. You might relate to my story in some way.

'I am telling you something personal and private about myself. You don't have to have a sad story. You don't have to think of a story where you have been down and came back up. You can have a great story, you don't always have to go from pain to pleasure, you can go from pleasure to bliss.'

So it is not like if you have a sad story, it will work well. You can say, 'You know what, I have been happy all my life and I see people who are sad all their life and I am going to show you how to be happy all your life, let me tell you about all the happy experiences I have gone through.' You can even talk about a big change in yourself and not a big incident. It can be a small thing that had a big impact on you.

The rapport is built when you give introduce yourself. Many things can help you here, for example, facts and figures (over the last five years I have worked with 200 people helping them take charge of their life; I have been to so many countries, I have worked with so and so people), make the story much more authentic; they lend credibility to your position.

Whenever you give an introduction, start with facts, figures and come up with a story showing your vulnerability. Vulnerability does not mean weakness, it means something personal because then people will like your story well. They feel that this person is willing to share because his stories are powerful. Let them know you trust them.

You have to make the audience think that you are no superstar and you are just an ordinary person.

Your life experience and the people you know is sufficient enough for you to earn the right to teach. You don't have to be a millionaire, you don't have to have written a book yet, you don't have to have anything as an enough proof. The kind of people who will come to your programme can be of the same level as you or maybe one, two or three steps behind. They come to your programme thinking that you will help them reach a certain point.

Why would people listen to you?

When I went to my first corporates to do my business, they didn't listen to me and when I sent them a copy of my book, they were interested. So, if you want to become really established, write 10 books. Ravi Sharma comes out with more books than he has breakfast. You can even go for ghost writing; there is nothing wrong with ghost writing till it's your content.

Ghost writing is of two types: first when they interview you and gain all the content from you and then reframe it; the other one is when you give them a topic and ask them to research the topic for you and come back to you with content and then you reframe it. Most people who have multiple books coming out superfast are definitely getting them ghost written.

People think their work is their experience and I say your life is your experience. Don't make your work your experience because what if you don't work? The content does not have to be so perfect; it is supposed to be fun. Once you know the stories, you can utilise them as content. You need to understand the right way to describe your story!

So when you say, 'When I was at school, I was bullied and it was really bad,' that is not so impactful compared to when I say, 'Every time I went around the corner, I saw that bully wearing that red shirt looking for me and I would run away and my heart would beat and I would think how am I going to do this.' Always give stories with outcomes.

You should never time your stories; your stories should be based on what outcome you are trying to give. You don't give stories because you have to give a story but you have to give a story because the story should have a meaning and that meaning should be relevant.

You don't have to be an expert to change someone's life. Go out there and gather as many stories as you can! Because all the greatest speakers in the world tell stories and all the trainers give content. All the greatest speakers in the world create experiences and trainers give content and content does nothing to anyone because experiences change your life. Don't give any content. If you read religious scriptures like the Bible, Quran or *Bhagwad Gita* and something like that, it's all about stories. Every religious scripture is all about stories because stories are powerful.

You can always quote stories from these scriptures. Every great speaker is a storyteller. Whenever you end the story, end it with a specific outcome so the audience knows that the story is for the audience. And this happens when you leave the audience with an outcome. Many people face this challenge – they will tell a story because they want you to know how good they are; rather it should be when you tell a story, it should be for the audience, if should be beneficial to them and you are just a part of that story.

A DAY LIKE THIS AFTER THE SUCCESS OF A SEMINAR. FEELING GREAT AND MORE RESPONSIBLE BECAUSE PEOPLE NOW LOOK UP TO ME AS SOMEONE WHO CAN BRING ABOUT CHANGE IN THEIR LIVES. THE CONVERSION IS 17%, YET ONLY 57 PEOPLE ATTENDED. WE DID A PRE-SCREENING CALL WITH THREE QUESTIONS ABOUT AGE, CAREER AND THE NEXT 5-YEAR PLAN, TO UNDERSTAND THE TRIBE. HAD THE RIGHT TRIBE IN THE ROOM.

SARITA CHAUHA, BUSINESS COACH

IT IS THE EDUCATION OF LIFE THAT SHAPES AN AMBITIOUS PERSON.

8

Do's and Don't's When on Stage

What to do on Stage

Let me tell you how to start a presentation, when you come on the stage, there is a certain format that you must follow. It will give you instant credibility and establish a rapport because, you are trying to influence people towards a certain way of thinking. When you are influencing people, the majority of your time, about 40% at least has to go into building rapport with people who start to relate to you.

And the best way for people to relate to you is through stories. If you say your story in a way people don't understand, if I am doing a seminar here on business and I tell you only about the struggles that I went through in my life, the business owner may not want to hear that. So, I have to make the story relevant to my tribe/audience. It cannot be a story just because it is a great story; and anyway, not all stories are great.

If I am selling a sauna belt, I am not going to give you a story about children. I want to give you stories about women and men who are overweight and who don't have time or the energy to exercise. So, your story has to be relevant, and the best way to give a story is to give your story and your story makes people connect.

What is your story? When you come on stage and introduce yourself, you have to remember that the objective is not to tell your story but to build a rapport. My story has not really changed much. I normally say, 'Hi, my name is

Arfeen Khan. I have been involved in this profession since 19, when I first started. When I was 19, I was completely broke, I failed my English three times, I failed my Mathematics three times, I didn't have a clue where I was going. What am I trying to say now? What am I telling you? Despite initial failure I was able to.

'I am like you, I am an ordinary guy. I am not someone born to be a speaker or a coach. I am less than an ordinary guy, I failed. I worked in Dominos, I worked in McDonalds, and I washed cars and I have done all kinds of work. So I tell my story and I let you know that I am the same like you. I am not extraordinary but when I was 19, my father asked me a question, he said, "Doing what you are doing now, where will you be in five years' time?" Hence, I named one of my book *Where Will you be in 5 Years' Time?* And I did not know where I was going to be; I had no idea and it scared me that in five years...forget five years I had no idea where I was going to be in next five weeks.

'So I gave myself a moment to think: 'What am I going to do in my life?' And all of a sudden I came across an opportunity, I started to do some business. From the age of 19 to 21, my whole life changed, I went from being an ordinary guy to being financially well off and above that, I was very confident. Nothing changed around me apart from me. what I am trying to say is that you can change too. I am actually telling you that I had nothing and I changed. You must be thinking in your mind, 'Wow, change is possible.' So I am trying to build a rapport with you, I am trying to speak of what is coming up.

'When I first started speaking, I was so nervous, I was petrified. I held a glass in my hand and my mic went into the glass – I was that nervous. What I am telling you here is nervousness is OK, you can be nervous. I could not speak,

I have never been taught to speak by anyone in my life. I never had anyone saying to me, "Do this and do that."

Now what I am telling you here is that you can be yourself, whoever you wish to be. You do not have to be somebody who has been given an image of a certain kind of speaker. You never come to stage and say, 'Hi friends.' You are not my friend because friends don't listen to each other.

The moment I say, 'Hey friends,' your brain would say he is my buddy and friends don't listen to each other, very rarely do they listen to each other. So you never say, 'Hi people,' you have to greet your audience saying, 'Good morning', 'Good afternoon', 'Good evening ladies and gentleman'. Respect, and after the initial moment, scan your audience and then stop; and there is nothing more powerful than a pause.

You come on stage, everyone claps and you stop and you look around at the audience. It's like 'I have arrived'; it gives you a chance also to get rid of your nervousness. I ground my feet, I imagine I am an Oak tree and I can be flexible but I am not going to move. There are many other points that you need to remember when you are on stage. I talk about it in detail in my Speak To a Fortune programme.

There used to be an encyclopedia called Encyclopedia Botanica. It was a 24-30 edition encyclopedia and maybe a 25-30 years ago or maybe earlier, they were for about 2000 pounds – that comes to around 2 lac rupees. About 25-30 years ago, that was a lot of money. But they were beautiful, if you wanted to find out something, you could get an encyclopedia and you could go through it. In the good old days, when you actually looked for information, you put some effort in, actually looked for it; found it and made notes. But to have an Encyclopedia Botanica was a dream. If someone came to your house and you had this Encyclopedia Botanica, you were royalty. It's like a Ferrari of knowledge.

And people would show it off in their lounge, it would be in a glass cabinet.

The moment someone walks in, it should be there! And guess who bought the Encyclopedia Botanica? Who were the most popular customers of Encyclopedia Botanica? Almost 90% of the customers who could not afford Encyclopedia Botanica. The rich would buy it, because for them it would be like buying anything and putting it in their library. But they did not go to many rich people. This was like the Rolls-Royce of education and this is how they sold it. They had 112 questions that they would ask the customer. As you walked in, they would say, 'It's a good morning' and of course, in return you would say, 'Yes it is.' Nobody is going to say no it's a bad morning.

So, they would keep asking questions and you would keep saying 'yes' to each question. They would build familiarity like they would say 'You are wearing a nice black shirt' and answer by you would be 'yes' and then they would say this would cost you 2000 pounds, all you have to do is pay in 3 installments, would you like to sign and they would say 'Yes'. Because you build familiarity, and the audience keeps saying 'yes'. In many seminars, transformational experts say, 'If you agree with me, say "yes". And how many times will they say 'yes'? A million times! There you go and that's how easy it is.

So you get on stage and then you tell your story. Your story has to be based on proof. What you are trying to say is this, 'I go on stage and I say "Ladies and gentlemen, thank you for coming this morning, and I think I should earn the right to talk to you from here. You have given me your time; you have given precious moments of your life to listen to me, why should you listen to me?

'Let me tell you my story' and the story should be full of facts, figures and things that are in common with the audience. How long should your story be? As long as people remain engaged. The good thing about a head nod is that when you nod your head, people start nodding. If you stand still, the audience becomes nervous, because they tend to match your reaction; it's a human nature to do so. You got to tell your facts, figures and commonalities, so people build a rapport. That's how you start a presentation. The next time you go on stage, ask questions, find your audience, and give your story in five minutes so you can build rapport with somebody.

What to Wear?

Talking about attire, if you are going to a corporate event wear a suit, otherwise you can wear casuals. Women anyway dress well, man dress awful. Choose good colours like black as it represents power, strength. Brown shoes and white socks are illegal; they should be banned forever. And you have to take care of your grooming really well, having huge patches of sweat under your arm is not allowed; that looks awful. Make sure you smell really good because people will come up to you and as a speaker you have to be really polished.

You can go up to your friends and ask them to check if you smell okay and that's completely fine, I am not joking. And if you have got crew members and they are running up and down with mics and as they are running if there is a whiff of rotten mushrooms, that's really awful and your audience will collapse.

You have to make sure your crew is really well taken care of. These are small things but they really make a difference. Nails for example; make sure you cut them and they are clean as people notice them. I once did a seminar and I had a long nail and people came to me saying why are your nails so dirty. When you come on the stage, you have to make sure you look the best person in the world. Polo shirts for men –

they are very smart. White shirt, grey shirt but you need to be very careful of the sweat patch.

When I first came to India, I travelled by train because in London everybody used to travel by train so I decided to travel by train. And I used to wear a suit and it used to be so funny and people used to stare. And then came the day when I reached for the train during the rush hour and it was a scary experience. Not because there were so many people but because there were so many armpits in my face. It was terrifying. So when you are walking in the audience, you have to smell good, you have to look good.

Like Hollywood actors or Bollywood actors, before they go on stage, they really groom themselves well. Get yourself a makeup man. When you become famous and well known, wear whatever you want and nobody will complain to you.

If you are unsure, wear a jacket and a suit and you are safe. It should not be a white or a pink or a green one, it should be a dark colour a grey, dark grey or black or dark blue with a white, blue or pink shirt, and you will look fantastic with black shoes and black socks, no white socks allowed. There will come a time when you can take seminars in shorts; you can do it from your day 1 also if that's the kind of image you want to give your audience. If your content is fabulous then people forget what you look like.

Talking about voice modulations, be yourself and have your own style. Otherwise when you start saying, 'Ladies and gentleman, welcome today' in enthusiasm booming voice and by not being yourself, and off stage if you are a soft spoken person, it doesn't work. Your personality on and off stage should be very similar. Maybe a little louder when you are on stage but there should be a similarity. You have to be relatively the same. It's not an act or performance. Many people come on stage and perform and their accent changes. Some people develop a remarkable accent. I have seen this and many of my friends do it. But you don't need an accent; your accent is good enough.

How to Express Yourself on Stage

When you are on stage, you have to express your emotions with your eyes, because your eyes are the projection system of your entire body. If I have to express any emotion, it should come from the eyes and the body takes care of itself. When you are telling a story, and the way you become effective, is by you expressing the emotion through your eyes and any story where the audience gets connected with you is when you express through your eyes.

Great actors like Al Pacino, Amitabh Bachchan, Dilip Kumar, Kamal Hassan, Paul Newman, Michael Knowles, Paresh Rawal, Irfan Khan, and Hrithik Roshan, all these actors express themselves marvellously with their eyes. If you have seen Amitabh Bachchan in Agneepath, even though he has got this voice and stuff but the main work is with his eyes.

Al Pacino is a short man, not a very big built, yet he is a very powerful and an amazing actor because he does it through eyes. I am not asking you to be an actor on stage. Because great actors never act, they just 'Be themselves'. They just are who they are and they express it.

All great speakers, trainers, coaches are very good at expressing themselves and they do it very naturally, they don't put effort in it. When you see a movie you can see that someone is acting and then there are movies where you feel: 'Wow! What a flawless performance.'

When you see *Mission Impossible* of Tom Cruise or other exaggerated movies with high-powered action, but how impactful are those scenes where you feel that it is really happening.

Shah Rukh Khan is a natural actor, he doesn't have much variety but that's fine because he is good at what he does. Whether he is running away with someone's wife or he is stealing someone's wife or breaking an engagement, the movie will be a hit. *Chak De India!* Could have been done by anyone and it would work, it was Indian hockey and the sportsmanship that won the movie. My perspective, Shah Rukh Khan is the biggest and he is the best, he is also one of the wealthiest actors in the world.

When we talk about Tom Hanks, what do you think of? He is the most lovable actor on earth.

When you are on stage and telling your story, you have to emote. Acting makes you less genuine when you are on stage. When someone says be happy you don't have to define happiness according to someone else because when you are real, people will feel it. You don't have to think, you just have to do it.

The more time you waste thinking about it, your brain freezes because of the pressure. Sometimes you just have to do it; either way, people are going to judge you, so it doesn't matter. You have to remember when you are telling a story, it is not a verbal act, it's an emotional act, and it's an act of you being able to express something.

We all have eyebrows and the real purpose of eyebrows is that it allows you to express. Without eyebrows your expressions go down dramatically. I don't have to worry about my voice modulation because my expressions will make my voice modulation happen automatically.

If you try to focus on your voice then the expression doesn't happen naturally. The voice comes naturally when you express naturally. So, when you are telling a story, use your body to get into the story, your story becomes more powerful. Sometimes when I do a seminar, I get really drained out because I have to express so much, especially when I am talking about stories that are very powerful or stories that are very emotional. You have to feel it when you share your story; the emotion should come out according to the way you feel.

If you have attended my programme 'Call of Destiny,' you will know that emotions are formed between three things – your body language, your focus and your language; these three combine to generate an emotion. If I want to be angry, I have to be in my mind in the right physiology and I have to focus on the right thing. Like I said, all great actors are so effortless that you don't know that they are acting. In my Speak To a Fortune programme, I have an exercise called expressing your emotions, which helps participants emote any emotion and understand how they can be in the right physiology on stage.

I watched a Russian movie last year and I walked out of the theatre. I hated it because everybody was acting in that movie and it was horrible. When you watch a movie like *3 Idiots* (2009), it is so natural, or something like a *Zindagi Na Milegi Dobara* (2011), it is not an 'acted' movie, it is just an ordinary movie, it is so amazing when they fly out of the plane, then they land and rejoice with each other. And you can feel it and that's what it is. Many of us get emotional when we watch a movie, and that happens because we put ourselves in that situation and we start picturising that.

Don't think a lot before you do because sometimes you just have to do things. Because when you plan something and it doesn't go according to the way you want to do it, it will destroy your flow. So, you have to be spontaneous enough to do something. Sometimes things will not happen the way you think but you should be prepared for that.

The combination of looking bad and being okay with it and not worrying about the opinions of people because is fine or else it will affect your performance instantly. Imagine running in the Olympics and not worrying about how good your shorts are looking or how people are judging the way you run or how you look compared to other people or what would people say if you lose. Your whole focus at that moment should be breasting the finishing tape.

I knew this acting and memory teacher from Mumbai and he wanted me to see him perform because he wanted my opinion. This person was an amazing memory teacher, he could learn a 30-page book front to back in half an hour and read it backwards. I was intrigued as to how he did it. One day he asked me if I could give a little talk about anything to his audience.

So I talked and I told them that acting is easy, anyone can do it. I asked three people to come to the front and emote anger and they tried to do it and it was really bad. I told them something that would help them express themselves better. And one of the people got so mad that he punched his fist on the wall. The teacher got mad at me and asked me why I was teaching them acting. And I said, 'I was not teaching them acting I was teaching them to emote. I do not know how to act.' And I smiled and was about to leave, but then all his students came up to me asking for my number because I made them emote in 10 minutes. However, I could not give them my number as that would have been unethical. What I am trying to say is that even acting teachers may stretch it but ultimately you have to become a great storyteller.

I met Rishi Kapoor once for lunch in Bandra and I remember him saying he hated all acting schools because he thought of them as bullshit. According to him, 'An actor is an actor and somebody who has to act will act. You don't have to be taught how to act, if you can emote you can act.' His son went to Lee Strasberg, America, and he was very angry that his son went there.

According to him, Ranbir didn't need it, as an actor he just had to emote, express and share and not be scared about it. When I did *Mere Brother ki Dulhan*, I was playing the role of an autistic and then there was a dance scene and I was thinking how to dance as an autistic person but I swear by god I never ever thought about the role I was playing, I just imagined myself as autistic and imagined what I would do and how I would be and how I would think and I would just go into a state because you don't have to act.

JUST FINISHED MY FIRST SEMINAR TODAY. SOME QUICK HIGHLIGHTS. TOTAL REGISTRATIONS: 400; TOTAL ATTENDEES: 50; DURATION: FULL-DAY PROGRAMME SOLD; LONG TERM (SIX MONTHS): SIGN-UPS; SALES: $5,000. ARFEEN KHAN, TODAY I FULFILLED MY COMMITMENT TO YOU OF DOING THE FIRST STF STUDENT SEMINAR IN DUBAI. COULDN'T HAVE DONE IT WITHOUT YOUR MENTORSHIP AND GUIDANCE.

RIZ RAZA, LIFE COACH

DEVELOP THE ABILITY TO CHANGE FROM WITHIN; THE ENTIRE LIFE AROUND YOU WILL CHANGE DRAMATICALLY.

9

How to Create Irresistible Offers

How to Make Your Tool?

What are the various tools you can use?

Look at your process step by step, the content you get. When you give content, there has to be something in it that you can automate or systemise. For example, assignment system can be a manual.

Suppose you make an app where every day you can download things, that's a tool. If you have five steps, then each step will have a process and a tool. If I give you 10 templates that are really tested and are ready to use, what is that? A process or tool. If I have 10 readymade web pages for you, all you have to do is fill in your seminar details. Is it a tool or process? It's a tool. If I say to you if I give you a home study programme which you can take and teach your staff members, is it a tool or process? It's a tool!

What I have done is, I have taken my content and converted it into a system. Games in a seminar are part of the process. But if I create a game for trainers, where you can search for what outcome you want from the game, that list of games that can give you the outcome will be provided, now is it a tool or process? It's a tool. And these kinds of things are not costly to make. You can have white label products, or you can look for tools already made by someone else.

I will give you an example; I have a goal-setting system, where I ask you to write down all your goals, no issues of money or time.

Step 1: Write a list of 50 things.

Step 2: I am giving you 10-15 mins, I want you to give each goal a number.

Step 3: Whatever number you give means years.

Step 4: Now you circle all the one-year goals that you have got and pick the top three and then give these a date.

Step 5: Then pick the top three goals for next three years, five years and ten years.

Step 6: Now you can convert it into a tool in seconds.

All I need you to do is go online and set this system. Write your goals, then pick your goals and the algorithm will know which one you picked, and it will automatically say 'Congratulations, these are your top three goals'. If you are giving a process in your seminar, you have the system then. Design your tools, develop ideas.

You can develop a tool, make people use it at the start of seminar and then post your programme which is say for three months. At the end of these three months, you can ask them to use the survey and show them the difference in their performance after attending your programme. Every step of your transformation, you can make a process and you can make a tool. Your tool can be your video series. The objective of this tool should be to produce the outcome of that step. There is no point adding a tool if it's of no value.

I am thinking to white label my assignment system, where my clients can use my ready system and put their name on it and purchase it from me. These assignments can be used for any programme. When I started with an assignment system, it was one assignment, then we added the commenting section within the assignment system and now I can go into individual assignments, check and mess around with them and put a comment and an e-mail is received by the person saying, 'Arfeen has checked your assignment and made a modification, come and check.' Next, we added a harassment tool, where if the assignment is not done, a voice message is sent, a text message is sent, a WhatsApp message is sent and an email is sent every three hours till the assignment is done.

We have an automated phone call that goes when one registers for my seminar, and then that person gets another call a day before the seminar to confirm their presence in the seminar, so people don't forget. And the person gets the option to press 1 for 'Yes' and 2 for 'No'. But the basic purpose is getting them excited about the seminar. We have experimented this already, you call, or you don't call, people are going to come for the seminar either which way if they are excited about it.

Your tool doesn't need to be only an online system; it can be like a journal also. You can make tools out of anything. It can be a blank journal and you could name it 'venting journal'. What you can do is, after your seminar, you can send highlights of the seminar to the people who registered but did not turn up for it. These highlights can be in the form of short videos that can be emailed to them. And once they are done with the videos, you can send them another e-mail which would give them a chance to meet you, since they have completed watching your video.

Give them two dates, they can choose from. Now it would be easier for you, because they have already seen your video and they are interested enough. I myself am doing a campaign only for the people who have seen 70% of my video. You can also offer a tool when they meet you, or a free assignment. 'All Access Gold Pass' that I have is also a tool, it has 150 videos. Everything in these videos is from my seminars and programmes.

For example, if the outcome is to get a strategy session, you can put together a five-step video, and the video should be specific to outcomes. If you going to market it, you need to find out if your tribe wants it. People have applied for your seminar, you have a heading and you have the programmes, so you can pick any one of the things that you want to fix and do a video series on that. For example, would you like to get clarity on something? Watch these 5 videos and it will give you clarity. And here you give two to three steps but you don't give too many details. It should have stories and experiences and over a period of these five videos, they should develop a rapport with you. They should feel you are really good. These videos can be around five to seven minutes each. They can be from your seminars. You have to link these videos to get a specified outcome.

Once you finish with one video, there should be excitement about what will be in the next video. If somebody goes through all your five videos, they are going to buy from you. These five videos are a seminar; you can put an offer at the end of the fifth video. When you are certain you have a product that is going to produce a result, you will be confident about it.

If you are working full time, and if you are not meeting three people a day, then somehow you are wasting your life. Three people a day means 90 people a month which means at least 10 sign ups. So your mission right now should be meeting at least three people on every day through strategy sessions.

If you have a six month or one-year programme and you have a two-day workshop and if someone is not buying the six-month programme, get them into the two-days' workshop and then upsell. You can always start with a high-end programme, then a two-day programme, then a book and lastly a badge. Don't offer free seminars, instead take strategy workshops and a meeting is part of the process. You should do network marketing; show three people a business opportunity in a day. Always pitch your seminars and programmes, exchange cards, send them a reminder e-mail and remind them about yourself. Later, share some of your quality content with them and if they start responding, you know they are interested.

The Price and Offers

The higher is the price of your programme, the longer should be the preview because it takes time to build rapport. Ideally, I would like to do a three-day preview but for a larger number of people, maybe 500 people at a time. If I have a 'Speak To A Fortune' preview for three days and free of charge, I have three days to prove that I know what I am talking about and then you can sell a much higher package.

Tony Robbins has a four-day preview, it is a paid one but comparatively very cheap. He is doing only one a year but the point I am trying to make is that the revenue made on that day is nothing; it's like nothing for what they are spending. In your eyes, it is an event but in the eyes of the marketer or the promoter or the speaker or the coach, it is a preview to other programmes.

It is a four-day preview, the first day is a shock day, something like a 'Fire walk'. The point is to offer a four-day preview and then the programme price can be raised and many people register, compared to a one-day preview.

In four days, you get enough time to build a rapport, to show them that you are really good at what you do and you get enough time to do your strategy sessions. You can judge if your story is working or not by looking at the audience, you can see their expressions and know if they are connected. If they are nodding their heads that means they are connected, so just watch the audience and you can know if they are engaged.

Your eyes should be on the audience, but you should know the outcome of your story even before you tell it. What most people do is they tell a story just because they want to tell their story. Your story will become really a long story if you are telling your story to make yourself look good, but when your story is about an outcome, your story has to end when the outcome is delivered.

What I am assuming is even if my introduction in my head is outcome driven, I will break it up for you. I always introduce myself and say I have worked in 43 counties with 600,000 people which means I am global, I have travelled and I have worked with many people, but when I was in school, I failed my English and my Mathematics 3 times. In fact, I have never passed.

Here the outcome is that I am ordinary and worse than most people in my audience, so, I am just letting everybody know that I am an ordinary guy. I have worked in Dominos and McDonalds and I have washed cars as well. If you look at my fingers you will get a proof of it.

Here I am saying that I have done my hard work and I have been there. I was not allowed to go out of the house till I was 18. I had to be back home by 9.00 in the evening no matter what happened; my dad would not let me out. I am saying that I have come from a relatively strict background, I don't say this in my story always but I share it sometimes. What I am trying to say here is that every statement of your story has an outcome.

If it is a strong story, it will have some outcome. You don't have to talk about failure or your life being miserable, you can talk about your life being great from the beginning as long as you add meaning to it. And your ETR (earn the right) changes on the basis of your audience.

For example, if I am with a crowd of businessmen, I will change my ETR and my story would be something about when I started selling pens at school with superhero tops and then I sold T-Shirts and then I sold Strawberry with cream illegally, then I used to sell leather jackets, so I can tell business stories if I want to.

Similarly, if I am talking about relationships, my story will be slightly different. If you look at my seminars from the beginning, my stories never change completely. I just keep adding to them. When I say I have worked with the most incredible people on earth and the most ordinary people, that means I am trying to say I have been everywhere. So your stories should have outcome, if they are outcome-driven you, will know when to stop.

Your format for your preview should be that you should create experiences and not Wikipedia. You have to build a rapport and then you can start building energy if it is a big seminar and then you introduce yourself and thank them for being at the seminar, acknowledge them. Next, you tell them what they are going to get out of this seminar and this is how you are getting them excited.

The reason why you talk about this first is that your story backs it up. And now you tell them your story which is full of outcomes. And here if you have six stages in your process, you will cover the first in detail just so that the audience knows what you are talking about and you go through the other five in lesser details. By doing this you are going through your system, the only difference being you don't tell how for the other five.

You tell them this is what you should do and leave them to think how. You don't tell them that but you do tell them through stories that I have done it and what tools and processes I have used. You make the audience think that you have a system and that you have told them a story about it, you have got a way to do it and you have got something to help them do it, so how are they going to do it.

And you keep talking about the programme throughout your seminar, you keep mentioning about the programme and make them eager to know and get that product. Make sure you give content because there should be something. Most seminars are selling festivals. But you must be different. Give them content and value for their time so they don't feel your programme was shitty or you didn't give them anything. Make them feel good about it.

You can reveal all the stages except for the sixth one and create curiosity for it and leave people wondering what that is. The story should express, 'I was where you are today, somewhere on this journey. And today, I have reached somewhere and I can help you reach where I am today,' and that should be the outcome of the story and nothing else. Some people in the room would have no education or money and they would think that you are too qualified and when you show that even you are ordinary, they will connect with you.

Why You Need a Preview

Now let's talk about the offer, your preview is not where people will end up with their stomachs full. It's like you know, my friend's sister was getting married and this caterer company said, 'Why don't you come and test the food?' So they invited us to someone else's wedding and said, 'Try the food,' and the food was nice but they only gave us a little bit of each dish so there was a desire to have more but we didn't have more.

This is exactly it. It says PREVIEW, not a seminar. It is not a place where you give breakthrough after breakthrough but it is a place where you can demonstrate a breakthrough after breakthrough if you want to. A preview has a problem and its solution. When you come to my preview, I make the offer the moment I step on the stage, using stories or breakthroughs or examples.

So if you think that the offer is the sale, you are mistaken. If I have done my job properly, that is before my actual price revelation, most people in their head think that this is something that they want to do. But there are a few challenges you need to go through.

Another challenge is great content that will create energy in the room. The next challenge is to get people in the room and that again is a huge problem. I know a trainer and he has been training for 15 years now, but he can't get more than 10 people in a room.

When I did my first NLP (Neuro-Linguistic Programme) practitioner programme, I had 70 people in the room and I don't know a single NLP person in India who has had 15-20 people in one batch. We all would like to have our rooms heaving with people. It is very important to ask for permission before offering your programme. When I take permission, your mind is open.

So, always in a PREVIEW

1. Start with the problem you are going to fix.
2. Talk about the solution.
3. Ask for permission.

About the Offer

Talk about benefits using stories, question and do not give content, don't start training them there, and don't give them new transformations. All you are going to do in your offer is giving stories one after the other. You can do a Breakthrough in the seminar, but not for everyone. You can show video testimonials during the offer and these should be no longer than 30 seconds and should talk about their transformation during the course and not of you as an individual. A testimonial should never ask to do a programme.

A testimonial should have the following:

- Name
- Background
- Before the programme
- After the programme

Or you can have testimonials about money, time, can I do it (because the biggest reason people don't join is because they don't think they can do it). The whole objective of a testimonial is to say if I can do it, you can do it too. And the reason why you need Background in your testimonials is for the people to relate. And you can let the testimonials play during the breaks. You can also play your promotional videos. I always give stories about all my participants in the offer and then I show the testimonials.

Video Testimonials are powerful and live testimonials are the best. The only problem with live testimonials is that you have no control over the speaker, and in a video you can plan and shoot it and get really good stories. Some videos have music in the background while people are giving testimonials.

If you make your participants intermingle with the audience then your programme is sold even better than you. If you have written testimonials, you can put the picture of the person on the slides along with their testimonial. You can edit your testimonials to cut them short. And in a seminar, the energy levels are supposed to be high before the offer, so, if someone came for testimonials and has a long story, that would be a problem because we want people to remember the 'after the programme' part.

How to Create an Offer

Everybody has a story! If you end the story well and if you give it a meaning, every story can be a great story. You have to tell your story in a way and get people actually there by using more descriptive language. What do they learn from this story and how do you turn it into your programme? You are not doing this to sell only but to transform.

So, when you are creating your offer, you need to follow a process your audience goes through; that's how you get them to agree and achieve the last stage – join your programme.

When you are about to make an offer and you share a story of transformation it should not be shallow, it has to be descriptive. You have to link the transformation to the programme you are offering and that is how people will associate the programme to the transformation. And when you make an offer about your programme and you promise to do something, people will relate to that story.

Before you start explaining about your seminar, you have to create the pain. It can be something like, 'I met someone and I worked with them for three days and in three days, there was an incredible transformation' and then you give some more stories and then you can say that they are lucky as those three days are about to come and then ask how many of them would love to have transformations like those.

Don't go straight to your workshop, talk a little bit about the pain and then transformation and then give the solution. The flow should be the problem, its solution and how you are going to deliver it in three days. Don't ask for permission for anything. You have to go into this mode of excitement and explain everything of how you are going to transform their lives.

While offering you can sit down or maybe walk in the audience and talk to people because otherwise it is just like you are lecturing people. Never make a negative reference to the audience. Don't use very simple language. For example, you can call your webinars power calls where people find transformation, the ones where people have breakthroughs. And here you can give a story. Give value to what you are offering.

Explain your system and share stories of breakthroughs. And for sure you need to have an offer on screen for it makes a difference. I never used to do that, but I do that now. You can even distribute the sheets and ask them to refer to it with you. Script your entire offer because then you can place your stories, you can add examples, you can add transformations, you can add bonuses and if you memorise it, it will be even better. Also, you can have notes and you can even read it out if you want and nobody is going to stop you.

Don't talk about the ingredients because nobody is going to remember them, nobody is interested in the delivery method; they are interested in the transformation. There should be a flow in your offer or else people will lose their way and won't remember what you were trying to offer.

You have to use descriptive words while making an offer. A video and a live event are very different: in a video you don't know what the feedback of the audience is. And each system has to have a specific name which is unique and exciting.

Then you can tell the price of the programme and also offer discounts for that day or maybe some bonuses for the first few people who register. Also tell them the worth of those bonuses and also the transformations that they are going to get. The bonuses are going to be mentioned in the seminar anyway. Additionally, explain to them the payment process that you are offering. You can offer more discounts on full payments. And then just ask them to fill up the form and enroll and end the programme.

All you have to do is simply mention what you are doing in your content and then re-mention it with some transformational stories. Nobody gives a damn about technical information. Whenever you make an offer, make it such that everybody in the room is eager to listen. And not everybody is interested in listening to the technical stuff; they want to listen to the fun stuff.

There are only two things that you need to finalise before you do your first ever event: one is that you should be clear about the three-month or six-month programme that you are offering and secondly, the offer should be well scripted. This shall help you confidently place your offer in front of your audience. When it comes to the offer, people start getting very nervous but if you have scripted it well with the bonuses, the stories and the transformations and everything in place then you can just literally read-speak it out.

**I FEEL PRIVILEDGED TO BE LED BY YOU,
AN AMAZING HUMAN BEING, A GREAT LEADER,
VISIONARY AND VERY GROUNDED MAN.
ARFEEN, YOUR GUIDANCE AND
CONSTANT PUSH HAVE HELPED ME
SHAPE MY DREAMS INTO REALITY.**

IRFAN NOORANI, BREAKTHROUGH & GROWTH STRATEGIST

BARRIERS EXIST ONLY IN THE MIND, AND THE POWER TO TRANSCEND THEM ALSO LIES IN THE MIND.

10

The Art of Selling

When you come to my SMB or COD programme, there's an art of selling. In today's world, the more you tell someone to do something, the more resistance will appear. That is why if you tell your children to do something, it's better that you suggest them something, than tell them something. And when they make a choice, they own the choice, and they will never forget.

The same happens with a customer. If you are selling a pen and say, 'This pen is an amazing pen, and look at the way it looks, look at the way it flows,' then it doesn't work. Instead, I can come and talk to you, 'Try this pen. I love the look of it. My great grandmother got me this pen, and it's really smooth. When I write with this, I feel really inspired.'

So, if I know that someone wants to be inspired and motivated, and wants to feel great, they're probably wondering 'Where do I get this pen from? I want this pen.' But I am not going to give them the pen. At the end of the day, I am going to say, 'I have got a few of these pens, anyone interested?' And they will go and buy one. I didn't directly sell it to them, but I suggested how good this pen is…

The greatest people in sales around the world never sell. They never sell, they share with people, or they suggest stories or ideas, meanings. People don't buy products, what do they buy? Experiences! Experience of writing! People buy a Mercedes Benz, or a Ferrari for its symbol. And you buy it, because it makes you feel powerful or strong, or you like it because it makes you feel like superman or a superwoman when you are driving in the car, and you also buy it as a status symbol.

If tomorrow, riding a bicycle became the status symbol of the elite, people would go and buy bicycles, because we don't buy the bicycle, but what it gives us. Similarly, people don't buy the seminars, they buy what you are going to give them.

How do I know what you are going to give them? What people do normally is spend 90% of their time talking about the ingredients of the course. So my course has five days, we give you this module, we give you this breakthrough. We give you this and that, etc.

Seeding

Everybody has a story! If you end the story well and if you give a meaning to it, every story can be a great story. You have to tell your story in a way and get people actually there by using more descriptive language and also seeding your transformation in that story. You are not doing this to only sell but to transform.

Whenever you start your seminar, you have to start with three opening questions. This will be actually six questions like: how many of you want to…how many of you don't…

As you get more experience in your work, you don't actually have to even ask these questions. I encourage this in the beginning to just get people involved and all this questions should be positive.

There is a gatekeeper in the mind that prevents people from attacking, selling and demanding. Nobody likes being told what to do and the gatekeeper is the one that says that nobody can tell me to buy. But if there is a distraction and then there is a sneak in, that is seeding; seeding basically means giving an indirect reference to a transformation that is linked to your programme. If you see me walking in the seminar with a cigarette in my hand, and a Ferrari turns up and a beautiful girl turns up, by this I am implying that if you smoke, then the Ferrari and the girl shall turn up, and you would look cool, and that is the reason why people smoke. The first time you ever smoked was because it is cool to smoke; there is no other reason. The reason why women started smoking, was to show men that what men do, women can do too.

Hanging around with great people has a profound effect on you. If you hang around with really amazing people, the flow of knowledge is amazing. I am so lucky I have got some really good friends that I can hang out with. They talk to me and they are really positive and they are good and it's like a mastermind. It's like a group of people who share information and it is so simple that when we meet, the information just flows because having good people around you is just the best way for you to ensure success very quickly. If you come for my Speak To a Fortune programme, we will work together and you will find that you can make really good friends.

So here I have given you an example of people hanging out together being good and at the end of my programme, I make reference to my mastermind meets and then I decide to form a group of people to meet every month and it's called speak to a fortune mastermind. Now I could make reference to it in the early part of the programme, not to the actual mastermind but to hanging around with people and now the brain will say I know what he is talking about, he shared this story and therefore this group must be about really amazing people and I want to be a part of this group.

Seeding is not making reference to your programme. Suppose if I am talking in my programme and if I say you need to meditate and I have this fantastic DVD that you can use, is that the right way to do it? No, because I am telling you to buy this. What I should do is? I was looking for a meditative process that would work, something that would help me achieve lalalala…and these are your tribe's pain points. And I would say, I have, over the years, discovered what meditation is worth and what meditation is not worth.

I have put together this amazing collection of meditation, every day I sit there and my friend sits there and we go through this meditation process and my life has never been the same again. And then you can give stories. And then you can give it names such as ascension meditation, it takes you to the next level. I have mentioned it now and I have linked that CD or that name to a transformation, so at the end when I say to you, that part of my system is this hard light ascension system, your brain will know what I am talking about. So, I have given value for that DVD in advance.

Let's take an example. Earlier I told you there is a main course and there are bonuses. Every bonus that I have, every main course have to be seeded into my content. What I am teaching you now is what will make you a multi-millionaire. I don't care how much content you have, I don't care how much knowledge you have. You can have all the knowledge in the world and you will never make a fortune unless you know this, and this is what advertisers do. They seed in a transformation.

Seeding is not plugging your programme.

What can seeding do? It means no switching into sales mode because seeding means you are selling from the beginning. No long sales presentation at the end because the sale is happening all the way through stories and examples. It relaxes your audience because it does not look like you are selling.

When I say selling, you have to do it in a very natural way where the audience would not know. Create hunger and desire in your audience without selling. Give immediate value and then reference where to get more.

Stories can make a deep and lasting emotional connection. Tell a story. Outline the results, then credit the results to a specific part of your programme. I teach

SUPER HAPPY! CONDUCTED A SEMINAR OF THREE HOURS FOR 120 PEOPLE. 44 HAVE REGISTERED AND PAID. THANK YOU ARFEEN FOR THE SHIFT IN ME.

PAVAN RC, CREATOR OF ACHIEVEMENT SCHOOL OF EDUCATION

FINDING YOUR GOAL
MAY TAKE TIME, BUT ONCE
IT'S IN FRONT OF YOU, IT
SHOULD BECOME
A CONSTANT TARGET.

11

Digital Marketing: Promoting Yourself and Your Services Online

I am going to share with you something that is going to be the process to particularly sell or promote anything online. What I am going to do right now is demonstrate how to use digital marketing aspects combining everything together to achieve an outcome that you want. But right now, I'll tell you about doing a seminar or promoting a one-to-one session or to promote a book or whatever else you want to.

Three-Step System to Growing Your Business through Digital Marketing

In the following pages, you are going to discover the system that will completely change your life. The system is simple, but powerful. Once you master it, your dream life will be at your fingertips. I know that might sound a bit hard to believe. Trust me: I have lived my life bombarded with crazy claim after crazy claim. I have heard it all in my four years as an Entrepreneur and Digital Marketer.

But what you are reading now is not hype, and it's not an exaggeration. It's a detailed system that has worked for me and for countless other people as well. What is the system? Let's begin. This system has only three main parts:

1. Traffic
2. Your opt-in page
3. Your auto-responder

Let's break each down in detail

Traffic

Imagine a quick example with me. Suppose you open up a physical store near your house. Your store will never make any money unless people walk through the door, right? That is obviously the first step. Well, the same thing applies to the Internet. When you launch your online business, you will never stand a chance to make a profit unless you get people to visit your website. We call this traffic. To paraphrase Kevin Costner's character in the movie *Field of Dreams*, 'If you build it, they will come.' This is absolutely not true when it comes to your online business. There are literally billions of pages on the Internet and most of them get no visitors; not even one.

Your Opt-In Page

Let's go back to the example of building a store. Obviously, if you go out and rent land, you would need to actually build the store, right? You would need shelves, desks, chairs, inventory, signs, lights, and so much more. This can end up costing you tens of thousands of dollars, if not more. Nothing changes when you move to building an online business. You still need somewhere people can actually go to. However, there is one big difference. You don't need thousands of dollars. You don't even need hundreds of dollars. You can get your business presence online within a few clicks, and for free! All you need to start turning your passion into pure profits is a one-page website. That's it. We call these sites opt-in pages. You will see why in just a minute.

The most amazing part is that these opt-in pages can be created without any technical experience. You never have to programme or write even a single line of code. All you have to do is use our automated system and click a few buttons. By the way, you never sell anything on these websites.

Opt-in pages have only one purpose: to convince your site visitor to give you his or her email address and subscribe to your email list. The simpler your opt-in pages are, the higher the conversion. If you try to get fancy and complicated, your conversions actually drop!

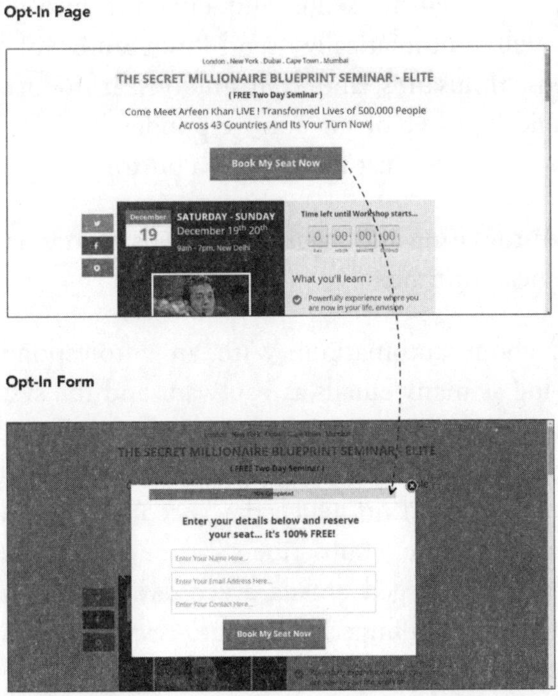

Auto-Responder

The email addresses you collect on your opt-in page don't sit on your own computer. These email addresses actually automatically fly into a database through just a copy-and-paste line of code you use. This database of emails is called an auto-responder.

There are many third-party companies out there that manage this entire process for you. They give you one line of code that you copy and paste into your opt-in page. From there, the emails are automatically placed into your auto- esponder. There are two major benefits to having an auto-responder.

1. Sending thousands of emails in a matter of seconds.

You just type out the email once (just as you would to a friend) and then hit 'send.' Suddenly, the auto-responder system will automatically send thousands of emails. Hundreds, thousands, and even millions; it doesn't matter. The magical power of an auto-responder is that you can email them all with just the click of a button.

2. Automating and logging hundreds of messages ahead of time.

Talk about automation! With an autoresponder, you can pre-log as many emails as you want and the system will start sending your new subscribers daily emails, all on its own. The system automatically remembers which subscriber joined your list and on which day. According to their day, thousands of different subscribers can be getting thousands of different pre-logged emails every day. All this without your having to lift a finger! These auto-responder services are available for a very small fee.

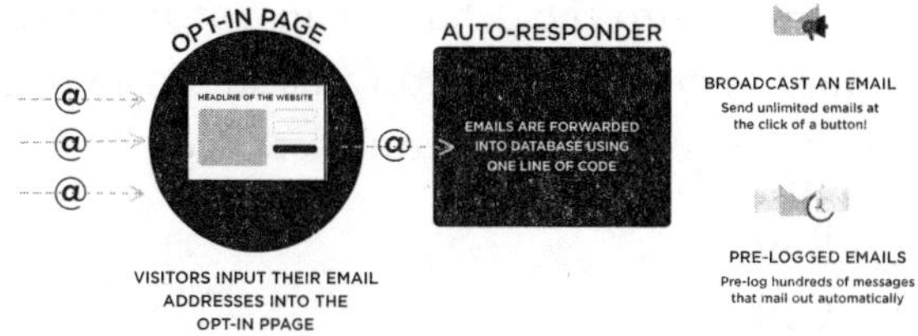

The larger your audience, the more sales you make. The more passionate they are about you and your message, the more sales you will make. The more sales you make, the larger you can afford to grow your audience (by re-investing in getting more traffic).

In order to get new fans to opt-in to your email list, you need to direct them to something called an opt-in page. This is where you basically bribe them with a free offer in exchange for their email address. The best part is that it is very easy to make this opt-in page. Remember, the simpler your opt-in page, the better your conversions will be.

Opt-In Page

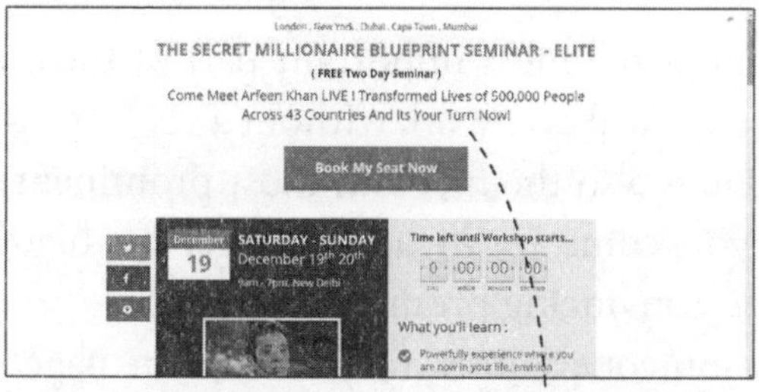

Opt-In Form

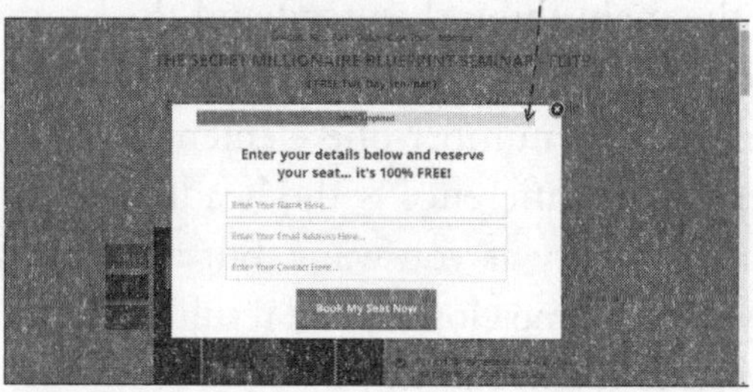

Now, let's dive into the details of an opt-in page.

If you want to create a high conversion opt-in page, there are only three elements to focus on the:

- Headline
- Free Gift
- Opt-In Box

Let's break down the three elements of a successful opt-in page:

Opt-In Page

1. Headline

The headline is the most important part of the opt-in page. No opt-in page will ever work without a very strong headline. The headline is also the first and most prominent thing you see when you come to an opt-in page. It's big, bold, and holds a very convincing promise.

When someone comes to your opt-in page, you have only a few seconds to grab them. Your headline should always be the main thing they read and the promise should be strong enough to stop them in their tracks. Years of testing has proven that the number-one element of an opt-in page that makes all the difference is the headline. You can make the graphics as pretty as you want, but the results of pretty graphics will not come close to the results you get with even a small tweak to the headline.

2. Free Gift

Decades of marketing research has proven over and over that the most powerful word in marketing is FREE. It does not matter what you are giving away; if it's free, people will line up around the block to get it!

Even to get someone to give you his or her email address, you have to be willing to offer something in return. Rarely will anyone want to give you something personal like their email address without getting something in return. Because of this, we simply use an opt-in page to offer a small bribe.

We offer to exchange amazing information for free if they give us their email address. In this example, we are offering to give them a free bonus. This report could just be a report of 10-20 page PDF file that takes us very little time to create. However, it is more than enough to convince someone to give you his or her email address.

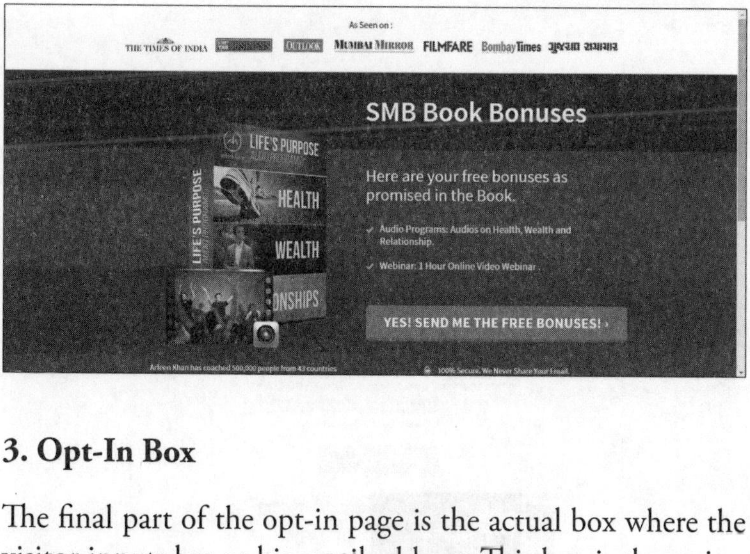

3. Opt-In Box

The final part of the opt-in page is the actual box where the visitor inputs her or his email address. This box is the easiest part of the process. You simply take the copy-and-paste code from your auto-responder company and paste it here. However, remember, without this box, the visitor's email address will never make it to your database.

I make it a goal to always make my opt-in boxes with some reinforcing text. I will take time to emphasise the free offer again and make sure I close the deal for sure.

Examples of Opt-In Pages

Example 1

Example 2

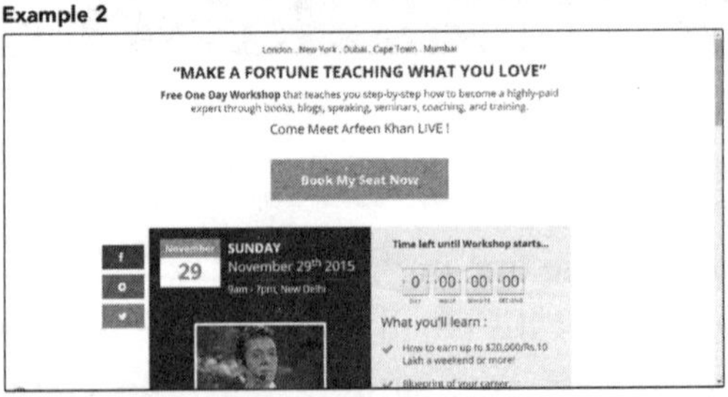

Example 3

Auto-Responder

With the help of your new opt-in page, you should have new subscribers flying into your email list. That's wonderful, but it takes more than just that to start making a profit. These subscribers are going to have to turn into raving fans who look at you as authority and take your advice seriously enough to make purchasing decisions based on your advice. That's where the profit comes in! To turn subscribers into fans, you need to actually communicate with them. That means you need to send them emails. This is precisely where your email auto-responder comes in. The invention of the auto-responder revolutionised online marketing. It automates everything involved with setting up and maintaining your email list. With an auto-responder, you can send emails to your audience in two ways.

- Pre-logged emails (based around the date they join your list).
- Broadcasting, or sending an email to all your subscribers at once.

When you use pre-logged emails, you can schedule emails ahead of time and the auto-responder system will automatically begin sending your subscribers emails. You can assign an email (that you only type once in your life) to go out immediately after the subscriber joins. The next one can be scheduled for one day after. The next, two days after. You have no limits; you could even schedule out 10 years if you really wanted!

When using the broadcasting feature, you simply log in to your auto-responder. You type your email (there are three types of emails, which we discuss in the next section) and you hit send. Now, it does not matter if you have 500 subscribers or 50,000; that's all you have to do. Every person on your list will receive that email.

How to Write Emails to Your Subscribers

There are two different types of emails you need to master. These two types of emails can be used for both the pre-logged emails and your broadcasting. I have always found it more profitable to focus on broadcasting rather than the pre-logged auto-responder emails.

I prefer to stay current with my list, talk about current events, and promote products with the most up-to-date sales message. That doesn't mean that I do not use the pre-logged emails feature. Every scenario is of course different; however, I typically use the pre-logged emails in the auto-responder for the first 10 days of a customer's subscription just to introduce myself. I use the pre-logged emails to build a relationship with my subscriber; I use it as a tool for them to get to know me. Of course, during the first 10 days, I also promote products to them; however, maybe not as hard as I will, once I start broadcasting to them.

So, once a person gives me his or her email address:

- Day 0-Day 10 = pre-logged emails (auto-responder)
- Day 11- Lifetime = Broadcasting

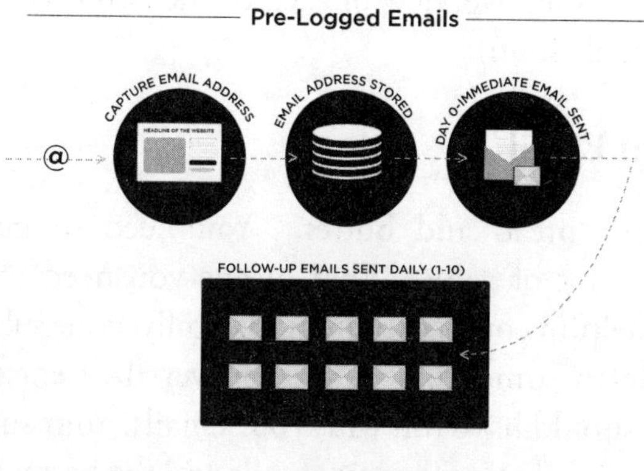

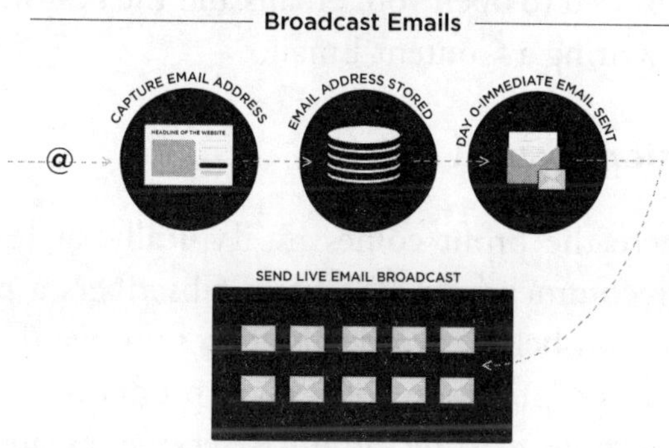

So, what are the two different types of emails that I recommend alternating? If you use this combination, you will build a strong relationship with your list and you will begin to profit incredibly fast! Remember, I recommend emailing your list as often as possible. There is a common misconception that if you mail your list less frequently, they will pay more attention.

This is simply not true and has been proven to be wrong many times. The two types of emails. When you sit down to write an email to your list, keep a healthy balance and rotate between the following two:

1. Content emails
2. Promotional emails

Here is a brief overview of each of the two (We will dive into the details soon):

1. Content Email

This is your bread and butter. You need to give your customers a lot of value. That means you need to deliver good and helpful content to them. Basically, your subscribers feel they learn something new whenever they engage with you. They should have fun with your emails. Your subscriber should be excited to open your emails and the best way to get there is by writing a Content Email.

2. Promotional Email

This is where the profit comes in. Typically, at least once a week, I recommend sending your subscribers a product/service that you believe will really help improve their lives. You can either promote your own products/services or you can promote existing products/services as an affiliate (meaning you receive a commission from the sale).

Track two variables in email:

1. Open Rate: Percentage of my list who opened my email.
2. Click Rate: Percentage of my list who clicked a link in my email

Quick-Profit Strategy

What if I told you that you could immediately start generating money from your list the second someone subscribes to your newsletter? That means that the instant someone gives you an email address, you can actually create a profit.

When someone enters an email address into your opt-in page, two things happen:

1. The email is sent to an auto-responder and stored in a database.

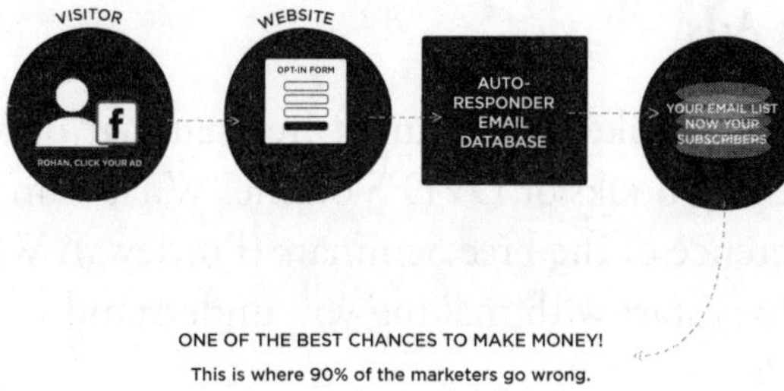

It's called a Thank You Page because typically, the page would thank someone for subscribing to the newsletter. About 90% of the time, it is a dead white page with a simple thank-you message. This is seriously one of the biggest mistakes made on the Internet!

Anyone would agree that the best time to sell something is when you have someone's attention. Here are two scenarios; try to imagine them:

A. Someone is doing a regular daily check of her email and she suddenly sees a small advertisement and clicks it. She passively clicks the ad to see what it is about.

B. Someone goes to your website, likes your first free offer and decides to give you his email address. He's eager to get the information you promised, so, as soon as he puts his email address in, he is eager to see what is on the other page. I think it goes without saying that you will have a much easier time selling someone in scenario B. The bottom line is that the person is paying attention to you! He has already said YES and shown that he trusts you. He is also fully engaged at that moment.

However, still so many marketers don't know that they can control the look and feel of the Thank You Page and they usually leave it like a boring standard one with just 'Thank You' written on it.

Facebook Ads

Start campaigns like promoting a free seminar or any such event or selling books or DVD'S online. What I am going to do is a reference of the Free Seminars (Previews). What I am going to do is start with making you understand:

- How to do the whole campaign
- How much money you will need to spend
- How many registrations you need to get
- How much conversions you want
- How many people you want in the room

For example, if we want 100 people in the room, for that how many registrations do we need for that whole seminar. Then we need to figure out how many people do we need to bring to our website for us to get that number of registrations. Also, how much money do we need to spend? And the number of days required breaking down and doing the whole thing.

The questions that start building in your head are:

- How do we design the ad?
- How do we create a website?

- Is it necessary to create a website in the beginning or an FB page is enough?

There are templates that you can use. But before you reach there, I will summarise the overview of how the whole process works and take it down step-by-step. Now when you talk about the whole process,

Part 1 is the FB ad.

Part 2 is the page you visit after you click on the ad. It is called the landing page, and when someone clicks on the page, it shows the details about the seminar.

And

Part 3 comes when you register for the seminar. You receive follow-up emails and maybe an SMS and phone calls as well. And this is managed by CRM. The CRM software means customer relation management which helps you communicate with the clients or the customers that you have.

I'll summarise the three-short-step formula for you:

Step 1: Facebook ad

Step 2: The page they visit

Step 3: Is the software we use to communicate via email, SMS or phone calls?

So, let's start with the Facebook ad…

How to create a Facebook ad

Let me explain the terms and processes of Facebook.

The first step is as soon as you log in, there will be one option – Advert manager. And when you click on that, you will see all the campaigns that you make. If you haven't done any campaign yet, this page will be blank.

On the same page, you will be able to see one icon mentioning Create advert. Once you click on that, you will see the Facebook objective. This is your marketing objective which means what you are trying to promote. And what we are doing here is trying to send people to our website or to buy a book or a strategy session which means we are sending traffic to the website. Always click on the traffic icon as when you click on that, it will ask you to give a campaign name. Ideally, I would recommend putting up a name of the session/product campaign that you are doing.

For example, your strategy session's name is Power Session Campaign, so you will put that as your campaign name. And suppose if it's a seminar, let's say The Speak To a Fortune, which is happening on 14 June, you will write Speak To a Fortune on 14 June. That's how you will put up your campaign name. So suppose when you have 100 campaigns by the end of two or three years, you will remember which campaign was specifically for what thing and then you click on Continue.

Facebook has 3 parts:

1. Objective of the campaign
2. Ad set
3. Ad copy

In the ad set part you will get quite a few details to fill in:

Location:
Age group:
Language:
Gender:
etc.

When you click on Create advert, it shows what you want to do – whether you have a product catalogue that you want to sell or you want to promote an app or you want to promote a video. And it will give you 10-15 options, but for now, you can select Traffic option because our objective in this example is to send people to the website. Select Traffic and continue.

This brings us to the second part, which is where Facebook will ask you all the details about your tribe.

Once you furnish that, it will show you whether you want to promote an app or a website. I will select website and the whole target market.

Now, it will ask you to show location, so I will type the location here and it will show you the potential reach which can vary from place to place. Now the geographical part is done!

The next step is selecting the age group: based on the age group you select, Facebook will calculate the number of people in that age group.

Now I can select the language. For people planning to take the seminar in Gujarati or any other language, the reach goes down again but we will not touch that for now.

Now the whole part comes about how much you know your tribe.

So you can narrow it down with:

What is the interest of your tribe, their hobbies what books do they read, what kind of magazines do they read, what kind of people they follow etc. etc.

This is all for your reference.

The more you know your tribe the better results you are going to get. This leads to the results that the more you know your tribe, the more you can engage with them and understand them.

Now remember, Facebook is not going to ask you that what are your interests and hobbies and so on. Let's say for us in the Speak To a Fortune programme, we do detailed targeting.

We target people who are authors, speakers or coaches, they read books like *The Secret* and follow people like Tony Robbins and this list goes on and on. We help our participants make their first campaign and teach the marketing tricks as a Bonus of the Speak To a Fortune programme.

There are a few things I absolutely love about getting traffic from Facebook:

1. No matter what niche you are in, Facebook has targeted traffic.
2. You can start generating traffic for as little as Rs. 500/day (or even less).
3. You can get your targeting very specific!
4. f done right, the traffic can be very inexpensive!

Facebook now has over 1.23 billion users. If Facebook were a country, it would be the third largest in the world. This is why I say no matter what topic you are building a list on, Facebook has millions of people you can quickly target. Facebook also has an impeccable and easy-to-use advertising system. It's one of the simplest ones I have ever seen. After logging in and initiating your advertising account (which takes 30 seconds), you have to simply fill out one page. On this page, you specify who you want to target and what you are willing to spend. That's it!

Facebook will then review your ad and your landing page. They have been known to approve ads in as little as 15 minutes or a maximum of 12 hours (from what I have seen). Here is what you are counting on when you advertise with Facebook:

You give Facebook a few targeting qualifications. These qualifications tell Facebook who your target customer is, and they will show your advertisement only to those people. Let's again assume that your ideal target visitor is represented by Rohan.

Rohan would log into Facebook at any time to simply check what is happening in his social world. As he scrolls through pages and pages of newsfeeds and pictures, he will start seeing small ads in various places. Suddenly, one catches his eye. Rohan finds the promise in the advertisement and clicks the ad. Rohan has now landed on your opt-in page!

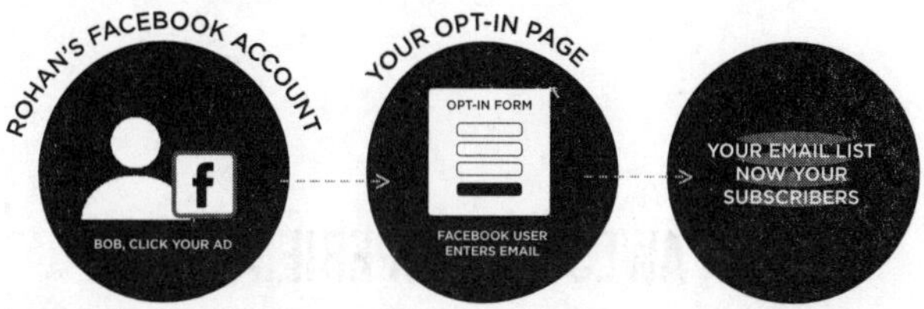

All in all, Facebook is great traffic to consider adding as soon as you can. Facebook is also very scalable from one place.

SUPER AWESOME EXPERIENCE IN MY FIRST SEMINAR. THANKS ARFEEN FOR ALL YOUR SUPPORT AND BELIEF IN ME. MY JOURNEY HAS BEGUN AND WHAT AN INCREDIBLE START.

RINKU SAWHNEY, LIFE TRANSFORMATIONAL COACH

DO NOT ALLOW ANYONE TO STEAL YOUR DREAMS. KEEP YOUR DREAMS. MAGNIFY YOUR DREAMS. ACT UPON THEM. MAKE YOUR DREAMS HAPPEN.

12

The Quick Checklist

- You should have some serious and exciting words in your vocabulary. You can go on Google and search for transformational words.
- Get a list of such words and even if people don't understand them, say them! It makes people feel good.
- Do not generalise your statements; be specific even if it is a goof up or a untrue statement; it makes the statement more authentic, the names make a difference.
- If you mention names while giving your stories, that adds power to it.
- Don't be very intense, sometimes you need to put up a smile and it makes a big difference. You don't have to be intense all the time, sometimes you need to chill a bit, you have to interact like a one-to-one, and you cannot just keep on going.
- Have your assessments in your hands, so, people can see there is something available physically, even if you have an online version. Have the assessment in your hand for people to see and make a conversation.
- Ask them questions, and make them realise how these assignments will help them.
- Don't give too much description about what you are going to do, keep it simple and short.

- You mention the price of your programme and then offer bonuses.
- Get your assignments ready before your preview, otherwise you won't be able to talk confidently about it, you will talk very vaguely about it because you yourself won't be clear about it.
- You have to be clear about what you are going to offer in your assignments for the people to judge. If you don't have it on board, you can't be confident about it, the audience can find that out.
- If you are going to say that the prices of the programme are going to go up, mention a deadline, mention the stepped-up price too, otherwise they won't believe you.
- Never ask how many people are interested in the programme.
- Make your offer, announce the price and end the programme by asking people to join you at the back for enrollments.
- Don't use an aggressive tone; be gentle while giving your seminar and have a smile on your face and that makes you a lot more believable.
- Be Yourself!

GREAT SUCCESS. CONDUCTED AN EVENT CALLED 'LEAD YOUR OWN RACE', WITH OVER 150 PEOPLE TURNING UP. THANK YOU ARFEEN.

UJJWAL ANDHARI, BUSINESS EXPERT

YOU DESERVE THE SUCCESS ONLY IF YOU ARE WILLING TO DO WHAT IT TAKES TO BE SUCCESSFUL.

Summary

If you limit your choices only to what seems possible or reasonable, you disconnect yourself from what you truly want, and all that is left is compromise. Robert Fritz

Everyone has their set of challenges, but I am not here to show you a way or to tell you what to do, it is your life and therefore, it should be your decision. But what I can help you with is, I can guide you. I can help you understand what I do for a living and make a fortune, and how you can do the same.

In life, we always come across choices. You get opportunities that you grab sometimes, and some you let go.

Opportunity

You can't always predict when an opportunity for success may come your way. Even if the opportunity presents itself, there is no way you can grab it unless you recognise it as a chance for yourself. What do you need to do to recognise and grab an opportunity when it arises?

First, you need to be able to make quick decisions. If you are too slow, you will most definitely let it pass you by. Secondly – and this is essential when you are making decisions – you need to be able to discard what you already have and be flexible to make immediate changes to adapt to this new situation. When you see an opportunity coming your way, you must be ready and have your hands free in order to grasp the chance.

So, maybe you can read this book as a sign of an opportunity that you can make a fortune teaching what you love! The next step is having the right mindset…

Mindset

Developing the right mindset is really crucial to succeed in anything. When I was switching my career in 2009 from my co-founded company to my new personal business, I knew there was a way for me. I kept looking, getting educated, testing, optimising – and I knew it would pay off eventually. I had a gut-feeling. And it did. I was on the right path. I had developed the right mindset. The next step is knowing your passion, what is the one subject that you would love to teach…

Subject

If you had to pick on one thing that you think you can do, then what do you think it would be? What would you do every single time? And of course you have to back it up with proof. When we ask for proof, the natural thing that people do is they start giving content and it is very natural for people to do that. Imagine I come to you and say, 'I believe' and you say, OK, where is your proof?' and I shout again, 'I still believe.' Instead if I gave you a proof, it makes me credible, it makes you viable.

So if you don't become an expert in one subject, or you don't build your story around it, you have to keep building your story over and over again till that story becomes so big that people talk about it. Not being able to provide proof, marks the difference between trainers and transformational experts. Trainers make no money, you can make a lac or maybe two lacs if you are lucky but transformational experts make a fortune. You must answer these

3 Questions For a Clear Idea of Your Subject

1. How can you help and serve others by helping in what way?

2. On what would others seek your advice?
3. What is your purpose?

Your Experience

If you come on stage with your subject and you are unsure and nervous, it means you don't believe you have earned the right to teach. If you are sure of yourself, that means it doesn't matter what the audience thinks of me because I know my subject very well. I'll give you the example of my ETR...

My name is Arfeen Khan. Over the last 20 years, I have trained over 6000 people in 47 countries. I am an author of four books now. I have worked with some incredible – people from those who have absolutely nothing, to the people who have everything. I have worked with celebrities, top corporates; I have had the privilege of going to an earthquake-hit zone, helping out. I have done a lot of charity work. I love helping people.

My goal in life is, in the next 10 years or five, I want to help 10 million people transform their life, have at least 10-15 books written and become absolutely known by face worldwide.

That is my little background. When I started my first business, I started a recruitment company. I got a job first, and then I stopped and started my business. In my first year of starting that Recruitment Company, I sold it for a million pounds. Prior to that, I joined a network marketing company. I sold water filters. I made 3 million pounds in that company as a young person. I then came to India and started a company here. In my first year, I did 250 cr of business starting from scratch. I failed dramatically after that, I have worked in the most difficult situations. In fact, for 1 year, I had no bank account. My bank accounts were frozen. I lived in an apartment with no furniture in India and I refused to go home until I had won my battles. The challenges were difficult but I refused to give up. In that time, not a single person in my environment knew that I was going through a trouble time. Because I was strong, powerful and not scared at all. I restarted my business and have done normally too well, much much better than I had done before.

I can take any person, in any situation to a great change. I have got 6,00,000 people that can help me do that. Would you come to my seminar?

I know you want to!

Your Programme

Name of the programme:
The objective of your programme is:
The outcome of the programme is:
What are the main sections of the programme?

So, it's quite a simple short template I have made for you. The next important step is Sales…

Selling

You don't have to sell hard, but you need to sell. An effective communicator is a person of influence. Now, influence is like a gun, it can be used to kill or it can be used to protect. Now, how you use it, is up to you!

So, when I started doing my programmes, I would market my products, at the end, nobody would buy them and yet they were good. Then I realised that when I listened to other speakers, they had really great art of actually selling their seminar without actually selling. The greatest people in sales, and around the world, never sell. They never sell, they share with people, or they suggest stories or ideas, meanings. People don't buy products, what do they buy? Experiences!

Marketing

Digital marketing is the marketing of products or services using digital technologies, mainly on the Internet, but also including mobile phones, display advertising, and any other digital medium. Wikipedia

From your website to the online tools–Facebook advertising, email marketing, online profiles, and beyond – form a part of digital marketing.

But not every digital marketer has a clear picture of how to use these tools to the optimum level.

Of course, you can!

So, if you don't keep waiting for a miracle to happen and make it happen and you have the right mindset, you can, just like me, make a fortune doing what you love!

Smash X Strategies – Overview

All of the SmashX Strategies Seminars are high energy, interactive and experiential events. The use of the latest technology and multimedia, along with Arfeen Khan's captivating presence, will engage you and ensure the ultimate experience.

- SPEAK TO A FORTUNE™
- THE SECRET MILLIONAIRE BLUEPRINT™
- INSTANT MILLIONAIRE BLUEPRINT™

We create custom seminars for corporates on request.
Visit: www.arfeenkhan.com

THE SECRET MILLIONAIRE BLUEPRINT™

The Secret Millionaire Blueprint™ seminar is based on Arfeen Khan's 25+ years of success in business, sales and marketing. The key to being rich is making it real in your mind first and then modelling and implementing proven systems for unlimited wealth. If you want to be on the inside track and learn how to think, act and become abundantly wealthy, not just financially, but in all areas of your life, then you must attend this programme.

During this event you will learn:

- The Secret Psychology of Wealth
- The Five Major Financial Habits of Millionaires
- The Root Cause to All Financial Difficulties and How to Overcome It
- The Millionaire's Strategy of Creating and Maintaining Wealth
- The Six Keys to Influence and Negotiation
- The Five Questions to Ask Before Making Any Investment

You will also master how to:

- Think and follow through like a millionaire.
- Manage your time and money to obtain maximum benefit from your efforts.
- Create a flawless and professional business plan.
- Boost the speed of your financial freedom through partnerships and joint ventures.
- Obtain the money you need for your product, business or service.
- Maintain values and ethics while building your empire.
- Attract abundance and success in all areas of your life.

For more information visit: www.arfeenkhan.com

SPEAK TO A FORTUNE™

THE SPEAK TO A FORTUNE seminar is based on Arfeen Khan's system that teaches you step-by-step how to become a highly-paid expert through books, blogs, speaking, seminars, coaching, and training. If you really wish to learn how to START, choose your topic, create your own transformational content, sell programmes and finally earn the income you have always wanted – then you should attend this programme.

During this event you will:

- Learn how to earn up to Rs. 10 lacs a weekend or more!
- Design a blueprint of your career.
- Know the magic of changing people's lives to be at their best and simultaneously grow your income.
- Experience a proven blueprint to market your seminars and yourself as a speaker/trainer.
- Learn how to bring your other products into limelight by building a lucrative brand.
- Learn how to acquire coaching/consulting clients.

You will also master:

- Designing a powerful programme from A-Z.
- Controlling the energy in the room.
- A proven blueprint to market your seminars and yourself as a speaker/trainer.
- How to use 'Accelerated Learning' techniques, so your participants learn faster and remember more.
- How to write a bestselling book – my 3rd book sold 50,000 copies in 2 months.

For More Information visit: www.arfeenkhan.com

INSTANT MILLIONAIRE BLUEPRINT™

INSTANT MILLIONAIRE BLUEPRINT seminar is based on Arfeen Khan's formula on how you can create a profitable funnel step-by-step and make money from doing business online.

During this event you will learn:

- How you can make a passive income thanks to Social Media Marketing.
- The proven six-step system to building, growing and exploding an online business.
- The single strategy used online to capture hundreds and thousands of leads.
- Steps to automate your entire online business, so that you can focus on what's important in your life.

You will also master:

- The critical important factors impacting the online business right now.
- How to create targeted campaigns that magnetically attract prospects ready to do business.
- A proven system that helps uncover the mystery of advertising to create compelling marketing without hiring outside help.

For more information visit: www.arfeenkhan.com

Notes

Notes

Notes

Notes

Notes

Notes

Notes